FORTRAN Programming for Windows

L. John Ribar

FORTRAN Programming
for Windows

Osborne **McGraw-Hill**

Berkeley New York St. Louis San Francisco
Auckland Bogotá Hamburg London Madrid
Mexico City Milan Montreal New Delhi Panama City
Paris São Paulo Singapore Sydney
Tokyo Toronto

Osborne **McGraw-Hill**
2600 Tenth Street
Berkeley, California 94710 U.S.A.

For information on translations and book distributors outside of the U.S.A., please write to Osborne **McGraw-Hill** at the above address.

FORTRAN Programming for WIndows

1234567890 DOC 99876543

ISBN 0-07-881908-3

Publisher	**Copy Editor**
Kenna S. Wood	Paul Medoff
Acquisitions Editor	**Proofreader**
William Pollock	Linda Medoff
Associate Editor	
Vicki Van Ausdall	**Computer Designer**
Technical Editor	Fred Lass
Greg Walters	
Developmental Editor	**Illustrator**
Jeff Pepper	Marla Shelasky
Project Editor	**Cover Design**
Nancy McLaughlin	Studio Silicon

*This book is dedicated to the heritage provided by
Louis and Helen Ribar and Philip and Arvilla Smart.
Without them, I wouldn't have been myself.*

Contents at a Glance

Contents

Acknowledgments

*I*n the creation of this book, I received a great deal of support and assistance from a number of people, including especially the following:

Bill Pollock, Jeff Pepper, and Vicki Van Ausdall at Osborne, who love to test my ability to write under stress, short term schedules, and moving targets. Of course, I appreciate their confidence. A great thanks also to Nancy McLaughlin, for her attitude and smile as we put this book to press—she was nothing but a joy to work with.

Dilip Wagle at Microsoft, for supplying the information needed along the way.

Peter Cross, Jeff Haley, and Ty Getz, who needed me on other projects, but who encouraged me anyway, hoping I'd learn enough in the process to make it worthwhile.

Most importantly, my family (Deborah, Louis, Jamie, Michael, and Leah), who sometimes aren't sure if they are living with a husband and dad, or an author. But for some reason, they always know the right thing to say so that I remember the difference.

Introduction

This book is not for the beginning FORTRAN programmer. It is for those of you who have used FORTRAN for a while, perhaps even a long while, and who are interested in using the new Windows environment for your programming.

FORTRAN has long enjoyed success as an engineering language, used to create programs with intense mathematical calculations, but with minimal user interfaces. Over the years, innovations in software development have come and gone, often leaving FORTRAN programmers with little to satisfy their appetites.

With the advent of Microsoft Windows and the latest, PC-based FORTRAN compilers from the likes of Microsoft and WATCOM, there are finally some new toys for FORTRAN programmers!

This book has been written to help you discover what Windows programming can mean for you, a practicing FORTRAN programmer. If you aren't using FORTRAN right now, that's okay too. The examples and applications shown in this book are basically compiler-independent.

What this means, of course, is that you should be able to take your current FORTRAN code, no matter what machine you have been using, and create modules that can be used on a PC under Windows. In the early chapters, you'll learn about specific FORTRAN compilers, focusing on how existing FORTRAN code can be used with the Microsoft and WATCOM compilers to create new Windows applications. In many cases, no code needs to be modified! Think of it...Windows programming without learning anything new except how to run the compiler!

Next, you'll learn how to create reusable code with Dynamic Link Libraries, or DLLs. The DLL feature is one of the most useful resources in Windows programming, so this information is used throughout the rest of the book.

DLLs are libraries that are not used by your application until the application actually runs. (Normally, libraries are connected to your program at compile and link time.) This system means that your applications can share libraries, allowing you to create smaller EXE files. And under Windows, only one copy of a DLL needs to be loaded, no matter how many applications want to use the functions contained therein.

In addition, DLLs have a standard method of interfacing with external programs. This flexibility will be covered in the latter half of the book, in which you'll discover how other programming languages can be used with FORTRAN. Specifically, you'll learn a little about the C programming language; then you'll see how a FORTRAN DLL can be called from C applications, and how a C DLL can be used from FORTRAN applications. The C language is steadily gaining popularity, and at least a reading knowledge of C is almost required for Windows-specific programming. You can rebuild your FORTRAN routines to run under Windows if you have no knowledge of C. If you want to read currently available books and articles that teach the details of Windows programming, however, you'll want to know the C language so that you understand most of the examples they include.

Later, you'll be introduced to the artistic aspects of Windows design, using a new type of programming environment called Visual Basic (VB). VB was designed from the outset to be an interactive design tool under Windows. Using visual representations of menus, windows, icons, etc., you first design the look of your program, and then attach code to places where it is required. This is very exciting for FORTRAN programmers— with minimal retraining, you can add state-of-the-art user interfaces to your FORTRAN applications and functions. All your FORTRAN routines can be compiled and used from within Visual Basic programs!

The reason that your FORTRAN routines can be made available to VB programs is the capability for creating dynamic link libraries. Using the

DLL feature, you can also link your FORTRAN routines with off-the-shelf Windows applications.

Using FORTRAN with off-the-shelf software is the next point of discussion. You'll learn about Microsoft Excel, one of the pre-written applications available under Windows that can use functions you have written in other languages, including FORTRAN! If you are using C or Visual Basic, you still need to write some program code in order to use the FORTRAN libraries you construct. Under Excel, however, you can simply use the library functions within any spreadsheets you might build.

Why is it helpful to use Excel as a front end for FORTRAN? Like other Windows-based programs, Excel provides all the tools you need for creating very professional user interfaces, including features that handle screen design and printer support. Excel helps you bring your FORTRAN applications into the newest realm of user interfacing, without the need to design all these tools on your own.

The final part of the book discusses the whys and wherefores of downsizing, or right-sizing, your applications. You'll consider the implications of deciding to move FORTRAN applications from your mainframe or minicomputer down to the PC level, as well as some of the pitfalls to watch for in these conversions. In addition, you'll learn about some tools that are available for downsizing. These tools help make older FORTRAN code more readable and maintainable; some of them even convert FORTRAN code to C or C++, if you want to follow that route.

The purpose of this book is to provide you with the background you need to help in making the downsizing and right-sizing decisions you may be faced with. As an added bonus, it offers valuable background information on how Windows applications can be developed, and how they can work together even if written in different languages!

Finally, after reading this book, you'll have a good feel for which programming environment you'll want to use under Windows. In many cases, you may just want to recompile your applications and use them as they are, with standard FORTRAN compilers, Windows' memory, and user-interfacing defaults. But when you want to start adding some of the Windows-specific features that are available, this book should give you a good idea of which environment makes the most sense for your applications.

Windows is one of the most exciting environments to become available to FORTRAN programmers in many, many years. In 1985, programming pull-down windows in VAX FORTRAN was something new and different. Not much has changed since then, as far as user-interfacing techniques for FORTRAN applications. Now is the time to move into the next generation, utilizing the Microsoft Windows platform with your tried-and-true FORTRAN code!

If you do decide to downsize your application to Windows and the PC, please write a note about your experiences to the author, at this address:

L. John Ribar, CCP
President
Picasso Software Group Ltd.
P.O. Box 7549
York, PA 17404

Welcome to the world of Windows!

Additional Sources of Information

*T*o enhance your discovery of FORTRAN at the PC level, Windows programming, C, C++, and Visual Basic, you have several products and sources of information at your disposal.

Software

Many existing FORTRAN compilers will not support Windows, but there are new FORTRAN compilers that will. Microsoft FORTRAN and WATCOM FORTRAN are discussed in this book.

If you are looking for help with Windows programming, you have many options. First, there is the Microsoft Windows Software Development Kit (SDK). If you need to access API functions, you may need to invest in the SDK. It was designed on the premise that users would program in C or C++, so you will have to work with C if you use the SDK.

There are several C and C++ compilers that you can use with Windows. The ones mentioned in this book, Microsoft C/C++ and Borland C++, will allow you to work with the API.

If you plan to use Excel as a front end, you may want to purchase the Microsoft Excel Software Developers Kit. It will also pay to get a copy of the professional version of Visual Basic if your plans are to build front ends to FORTRAN applications under Windows.

Books

Fortunately, there are numerous books on Windows programming. You should be able to find some at any good technical bookstore. Make sure that the book you buy is up-to-date.

There are a lot of books on FORTRAN, but not much material exists on converting FORTRAN to Windows. Most of the FORTRAN books are college texts or professional books, so your best bet is to try a bookstore at a local engineering school, or to call any of the major college publishers. There is a book available called *From FORTRAN to C* (by James F. Kerrigan, Windcrest McGraw-Hill, 1991).

If you want to learn C, C++ or Visual Basic, you will find a variety of books in any bookstore that carries computer books. Osborne/McGraw-Hill has been a leading publisher in this area for years. Their most recent books include *C DiskTutor* (by L. John Ribar, 1992), *C++ Programming for Windows* (by Anthony Porter, 1993), and *Visual Basic 2 for Windows Inside and Out* (by Gary Cornell, 1993). These are just a few of the many books available. Be sure to select a book well-suited to your background.

Magazines, Newsletters, and Training

There are several magazines and newsletters for Windows developers. Some of the better ones are listed here:

☐ *Windows/DOS Developer's Journal.* Published Monthly. For more information, contact:

Windows/DOS Developer's Journal
1601 W. 23rd St., Suite 200
Lawrence, KS 66046-9950

This is a good magazine for those who are developing for the Windows and DOS environments.

❑ *Windows Magazine.* Published monthly. For more information, contact:

Windows Magazine
P.O. Box 58647
Boulder, CO 80321-8647

This is an excellent magazine for tracking the state of Windows-based hardware and software.

❑ *Windows Tech Journal.* Published monthly. For more information, contact:

Windows Tech Journal
P.O. Box 70087
Eugene, OR 97401-9943

If you plan to take up Windows programming, this is the first magazine you should consider subscribing to.

You should also contact Microsoft University to check their current course offerings. You may find classes specifically geared to your needs.

Microsoft University
10700 Northup Way
Bellevue, WA 98004-1447
(206) 828-1507

Vendors of FORTRAN Tools

This is not a complete list of every FORTRAN vendor ever known. However, it is a representative list of vendors who are currently supporting and marketing their wares to FORTRAN programmers:

Products	Vendors
Blinker	Blinkinc P.O. Box 7154 Richmond, VA 23221
FOR_STRUCT FOR_C FOR_C++	Cobalt Blue, Inc. 875 Old Roswell Road Suite 400-D Roswell, GA 30076 (404) 518-1116
FORTEX	Dynetics P.O. Drawer B Huntsville, AL 35814
F77 Compilers	Lahey Computer Systems, Inc. P.O. Box 6091 Incline Village, NV 89450 (702) 831-2500
Microsoft FORTRAN Microsoft C/C++ Microsoft Windows Microsoft Excel Visual Basic	Microsoft Corporation One Microsoft Way Redmond, WA 98052 (206) 882-8080
plusFORT Fortran 90 Fortran 77 Interacter	Polyhedron Software Ltd. Linden House 93 High Street Standlake, WITNEY, OX8 7RH United Kingdom (44) 0865-300579
FORTRAN Tools FORWARN	Quibus Enterprises, Inc. 3340 Marble Terrace Colorado Springs, CO 80906 (719) 527-1384

Products	**Vendors**
Hi-Screen Pro II	Softway, Inc. 185 Berry St., Suite 5411 San Francisco, CA 94107 (415) 896-0708
FastGraph	Ted Gruber Software P.O. Box 13408 Las Vegas, NV 89112 (702) 735-1980
WATCOM FORTRAN WATCOM C	WATCOM Systems Inc. 415 Phillip Street Waterloo, Ontario CANADA (519) 886-3700

CHAPTER

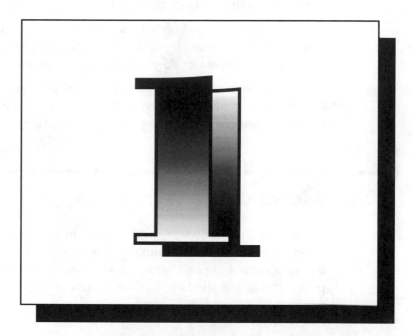

The Windows Programming Environment

*F*ORTRAN has long been known as the software workhorse of the engineering industry. Engineers use it for creating a variety of number-intensive programs in industries ranging from aerospace to accounting. FORTRAN has been known as a language that handles numbers well. It has not, however, had a reputation for creating the most user-friendly, or programmer-friendly, applications.

With the advent of Microsoft Windows and advanced programming techniques utilizing menus, mice, and graphics that made programs simpler to use, a change was needed. The newest DOS FORTRAN compilers let FORTRAN programmers apply the latest technologies for user interfacing to their tried-and-proven numerical algorithms.

This book will take you from a text-mode FORTRAN base into the new world of programming for Windows, a graphical user interface that adds a new level of usability to your existing programs.

The purpose of this chapter is to introduce to you the concepts behind Windows programming and the tools available for FORTRAN program-mers to move them into the programming environments of the 1990s.

Using Microsoft Windows

Microsoft Windows is a graphical user interface (GUI), designed to make using computers simpler, and maybe even more fun. In addition, the programming community is developing standards for how Windows programs (also called applications) should look and act. Because of this uniformity, users are able to work with multiple applications without extensive retraining.

Windows also supports some features not available under DOS, including multitasking and virtual program space. What this means is that you can have several programs running at the same time, and, if one of them aborts for some reason, the rest of the applications continue their processing.

 Note   In Windows, multitasking is performed with a *non-preemptive* scheduler; this means that several applications can run at the same time, sharing the processor, as long as they "take turns." This forces you, as the programmer, to add points in your program where you will give up

control temporarily. In other operating systems, programs are inter-
rupted by the operating system itself to force sharing of the processor.

Windows also supports an extremely large memory space. Even if you
do not want to add Windows-specific functionality to your programs,
running mainframe programs under Windows allows for use of this
extensive memory space. Under DOS, remember, only 640K of memory
is normally available to your programs.

Windows handles access to all the hardware connected to your
machine. You no longer access screen memory directly, for instance.
Instead, your programs link with the Windows API (Application Programming Interface), a set of routines that allows Windows to interact with
the hardware. As a result, your programs can run on any computer that
supports Windows, and all you have to do is support the generic Windows
libraries.

Another leap forward for Windows has been the introduction of
Dynamic Link Libraries (DLLs). When you create applications that use
DLLs, the programs do not actually link in the library code until the
program is run. In addition, multiple applications can share a DLL's code,
conserving both memory and disk space. DLLs are discussed more fully
in Chapter 5.

Two drawbacks have historically stunted development of applications
for Windows. First, there was always a requirement to purchase the
Windows Software Development Kit (SDK). The kit was originally quite
expensive, and many developers could not justify the cost. Now, the cost
has come down, and many compilers (including the Microsoft and
WATCOM FORTRAN compilers) include the tools you need for developing
Windows applications without the need for the SDK.

The second drawback for Windows development has been the cost of
the hardware required. A serious Windows developer will want an 80486
computer with at least 8 megabytes of memory, a 200Mb hard disk, and
Super VGA color graphics. Windows will run on much less, but perfor-
mance suffers. The prices keep falling, and now are at a point where
Microsoft can sell more than one million copies of Windows in a month!
The market is here, and you can be part of it with your FORTRAN
applications.

FORTRAN Compilers and Tools for Windows

There are two major FORTRAN compiler vendors who support actual Windows programming: Microsoft and WATCOM.

Microsoft FORTRAN supports building applications and DLLs using FORTRAN. To allow better use of existing code, a large number of VAX and IBM extensions have been added to the compiler (see Chapter 2 for more information on these extensions). The Windows API is not supported directly, but a set of libraries, known as QuickWin, allows building simple FORTRAN user interfaces for Windows (covered in Chapter 3). In addition, DLLs of FORTRAN code can be built, and interfaces with other languages are also available for adding more advanced user interaction.

In addition to supporting the creation of applications and DLLs under Windows using standard FORTRAN code, WATCOM provides access to the complete set of Windows API functions. WATCOM is discussed in Chapter 4.

There are also other tools that will help you write Windows programs. Tools to help update older FORTRAN code to newer structured programming techniques are discussed in Chapter 9. Other tools that allow you to create C or C++ code from FORTRAN code are covered in Chapter 6, as part of the discussion of mixed-language programming.

The Windows Programming Environment

The programming environment is different in Windows than in most other development arenas. There are new file types to use, new ways of looking at libraries, and new ways to interface applications with other applications.

The current FORTRAN compilers have you enter your programs in DOS text-mode programs. Once you have an application written, you compile and link it in DOS. Then, you can run the final application in Windows. To run a Windows program called MYPROG.EXE from the DOS command line, you would type **WIN MYPROG.** This command starts Windows (WIN) and MYPROG.EXE (MYPROG) at the same time.

If you are already running Windows, you can start a program by selecting the File menu from the Program Manager, selecting Run from the File menu (see Figure 1-1), and typing in the name of the program you want to run.

If your program is represented by an icon, you can double-click on the icon, and the program will run.

The Windows API Interface

The Windows API provides routines for handling most standard Windows functions, including management of the screen, keyboard, and mouse. There are also routines for controlling memory, file management and communications. These functions are provided within the Windows environment, so all applications can share them without each program being weighed down with a copy of the code.

Running a program from within Windows

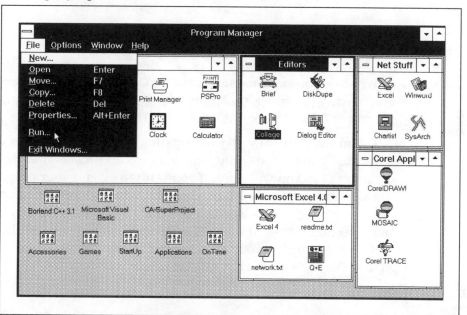

Microsoft FORTRAN does not directly support the Windows API. You can use the QuickWin library to write programs that use simple user-interfacing routines (like OPEN, READ, and WRITE). As an alternative, you could write API calls using Microsoft C/C++, and then link these with your FORTRAN code. WATCOM supports the full Windows API.

Another method for accessing the Windows API is through the connection of your FORTRAN code to other programs that already use the API. For instance, Microsoft Excel is a spreadsheet application that can call FORTRAN functions embedded in DLLs. (This process is covered in Chapter 8.) The ability to connect your programs in this way lets you create applications within Excel that handle all user interaction and printing, but that use your FORTRAN functions to perform calculations.

Other languages, such as Microsoft Visual Basic, have the tools to create user interfaces for Windows. As with Excel, you can then attach your FORTRAN functions for use within the new environment. This type of interface is described in Chapter 7.

The good news is that there is a standard interface growing. By using DLLs and Windows calls, you can provide other applications with access to your tried and true FORTRAN routines. In the same way, routines from others can be used to enhance your programs, without worrying about the original language or compiler used.

Tools of the Trade

What do you need to start writing FORTRAN programs for Windows? You need a compiler that supports Windows programming, such as Microsoft FORTRAN or WATCOM FORTRAN F77.

If you want to convert your existing FORTRAN routines to DLLs or write full applications that only require text-mode user interfaces, a compiler is all you will need. If you want to extend your programs using the Windows API, you will need a good Windows reference book or two. For some suggestions, see the section, "Additional Sources of Information," located at the front of this book. If you are using the Microsoft FORTRAN compiler, you will also need an additional compiler (C/C++ or Visual Basic) to access the API functions.

If you plan to do serious Windows development, additional tools will be required, including a resource compiler, help compiler, dialog editor, and icon editor. You may wish to purchase the Windows SDK if your compiler doesn't include the tools you'll need. You may also want a Windows-based editor and debugger (WATCOM does include a Windows-based debugger, and Microsoft CodeView for Windows is also available).

One tool provided with both compilers is a Make utility. Make is used to recompile and build your application, based on a makefile script. The Make utility becomes necessary as more and more files, and types of files, are used to create your applications. It is no longer a world of compiling a single file to generate an application. There are now definition files, resource files, library files, and your original source code. A makefile automates the process of building your application, performing only the parts of the process that are necessary. Makefiles are covered in-depth in the manuals provided with your compiler.

 Note   Please take the previous paragraph with a grain of salt. Both the Microsoft and WATCOM compilers still allow a Windows program to be built by a compile-and-link command, using your single source file. However, full-blown, Windows API-based, GUI-oriented programs can involve many files. These complex, powerful programs are where Make becomes extremely useful.

What About C or C++?

For years, all the source code examples for Windows programs have been shown in the C language. This tradition is changing, as many other compilers are now available for Windows programming. However, much of the source code available is for C, or more recently for C++, an object-oriented version of C.

Do you need to learn C to program under Windows? Probably not. As mentioned previously, your FORTRAN code can run under Windows, and there are applications available to use as front ends for a nicer user interface. However, you may wish to acquire at least a reading knowledge of C. Since there is so much code available in C for Windows, you can certainly broaden your own understanding by having that ability.

Certainly, moving all your existing FORTRAN code to C could be a major investment. There are ways of reducing this work, however, and you'll learn about them in Chapters 6 and 9.

Where Do You Go from Here?

You have probably decided that Windows is worth looking into for your FORTRAN code, which is why you bought this book. What should you do next? Start here, and you'll be writing FORTRAN programs for Windows in no time.

What This Book Will Cover

The flow of this book is from the basics of FORTRAN through the use of other applications that you can use for generating FORTRAN-aware programs. Chapters 2, 3, and 4 cover the specifics of the Microsoft and WATCOM FORTRAN compilers.

Chapter 5 teaches you about Dynamic Link Libraries, what they are used for, why you will want to use them, how to create them, and how to use them from your applications.

In Chapter 6, you'll learn a little about C and C++, and how applications and DLLs written in FORTRAN and C/C++ can share both data and program code. This sharing is one way in which programmers can extend the usefulness of their FORTRAN code.

Next, in Chapter 7, you'll learn about Visual Basic, another programming language. What makes Visual Basic different is that it was designed from the ground up to be a Windows programming language and environment. Using Visual Basic, you can generate some wonderful front-end applications for your FORTRAN routines. This means that the Visual Basic program will be the part of your application that the user will see; it will interact with the user to handle all input and output of data, but will call your FORTRAN routines to perform the calculations.

In Chapter 8, you'll learn about using your FORTRAN routines with applications that are available off the shelf from different software vendors. In the discussion of Excel, you'll learn how to call routines in a FORTRAN DLL from within such applications, even when you have no knowledge of the source language or compiler used.

Finally, Chapter 9 delves into the process of in *downsizing*; that is, converting FORTRAN code that was originally written for a mainframe or microcomputer platform to run on personal computers. Some of the tools available for downsizing will be covered, as well as the pros and cons of making such a conversion.

The Next Step

Install Windows and FORTRAN on your computer. Try the examples in this book, and before long you'll be writing Windows programs! Then, if the taste of Windows catches your fancy, examine the "Additional Sources of Information" section at the beginning of this book for resources and tools to help propel your programming exploits even further.

CHAPTER

Introduction to Microsoft FORTRAN 5.1

*I*f you are planning to convert FORTRAN code to the Windows platform, Microsoft FORTRAN offers many tools to significantly enhance your programs with little overhead. Microsoft FORTRAN can make writing graphic applications much simpler. FORTRAN programmers can take advantage of the tools in the Microsoft package to greatly enhance their code. The newest versions of Microsoft FORTRAN allow FORTRAN programmers to use the latest technologies of user interfacing with their tried and proven numerical algorithms. This chapter and the next will present many of the elements that you will need as you program for Windows. In particular, this chapter will show you how easy it is to run your current FORTRAN programs under Windows.

Microsoft FORTRAN 5.1 allows you to move much of your existing FORTRAN code into the Windows programming arena. While the full range of programming features available to C and C++ programmers is not available in FORTRAN, many tools exist to help you start making your move to Windows. In addition, links with other languages (C, C++, Pascal, and BASIC) and with application programs (such as spreadsheets and database managers) allow you to use FORTRAN code that has been proven over the years with the newer user interface tools now available.

There are two ways to use the FORTRAN compiler: from the Programmer's Workbench (PWB) and from the DOS command line. The PWB is a text-mode program from which you edit, compile, and debug your programs. Once you have built your programs, you can also run them; PWB will automatically load Windows for you first!

If you prefer to work from the command line, FL is the version of the compiler you will use. In the next sections, you'll see how to use both of these programs.

For more information on the FORTRAN language or the tools supplied with the Microsoft compiler, check into the Microsoft FORTRAN programming manuals.

Using the Programmer's Workbench

The Programmer's Workbench is a program development utility supplied with most of the Microsoft compilers. You first use it to enter or edit your programs. Suppose you have this small program:

```
      PROGRAM Power
C
C     Simple FORTRAN Program to calculate
C     the result of raising one number to the power
C     of another.
C
C     By:       L. John Ribar
C     Date:     12 Sept 1994
C     System:   Microsoft FORTRAN 5.1
C     OS:       DOS and Windows
C

      INTEGER*2    I, J

      I = 10
      J = I ** 3

      WRITE (*,10)
      READ (*,100) I
      WRITE (*,11)
      READ (*,100) J
      WRITE (*,12) I, J, I**J

10    FORMAT(' Enter the number to be raised: ')
11    FORMAT(' Enter the power to use: ')
12    FORMAT(' ',I4,' to the ',I4,' power is ',I6)
100   FORMAT(I4)

      END
```

To start up the Programmer's Workbench, simply type **PWB** at the DOS command line. Then create a new program file by pressing ALT-F (for File) and N (for New), or by choosing these items with your mouse. A new, blank window will open to contain your file. As you type in the code, the screen will look like Figure 2-1.

After you type a program in, you can save it to disk by pressing ALT-F (File) and S (Save). To open a file that you have previously created, use ALT-F (File) and O (Open). The PWB also allows you to have more than one file open at a time. This can be very handy when you are writing large, multifile programs. With several files open, the PWB screen might look like Figure 2-2.

Once you have entered your program, press ALT-O (Options) and B (to specify the Build options). Then press ALT-S (Set Initial Build Options),

FIGURE
2-1

The Programmer's Workbench editor at work

```
 File   Edit   View   Search   Make   Run   Options   Browse              Help
                              C:\BOOKS\4\power.for
        PROGRAM Power

        INTEGER*2     I, J

        I = 10
        J = I ** 3

        WRITE (*,10)
        READ (*,100) I
        WRITE (*,11)
        READ (*,100) J
        WRITE (*,12) I, J, I**J

10      FORMAT(' Enter the number to be raised: ')
11      FORMAT(' Enter the power to use: ')
12      FORMAT(' ',I4,' to the ',I4,' power is ',I6)
100     FORMAT(I4)

        END

<General Help> <F1=Help> <Alt=Menu>                     |fortran        N 00003.007
```

FIGURE
2-2

Editing several files in the PWB

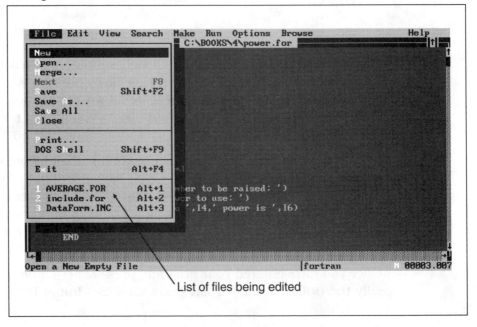

List of files being edited

and you'll be presented with a screen that looks like Figure 2-3. From here you can select the type of executable file you wish to create. The most common files you might build are DOS EXE files, Windows EXE files, and Windows DLL (Dynamic Link Library) files.

First, try using the program shown previously, and compile it as a DOS EXE program. To create your program, press ALT-M and either C (to compile the current program file) or B (to build the executable program, a process which includes all compilation and linking that might be necessary).

 Note Keep in mind that the programs shown in this book have been recompiled to run under Windows with *no* changes!

When you run the program (using ALT-R for Run, and E for Execute), you'll see a standard text program output, similar to that shown here:

```
Enter the number to be raised:
7
Enter the power to use:
3
    7 to the    3 power is      343
```

FIGURE
2-3

Selecting compilation options

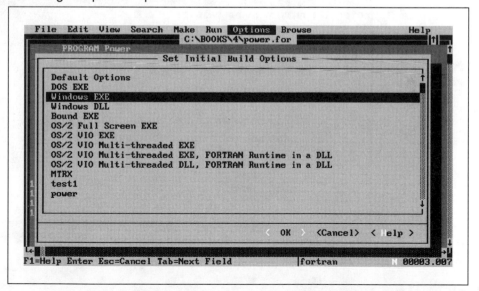

This should not surprise you. What might be surprising, however, is that by simply changing the compilation option (using ALT-O for Options, B for Build Options, and S for Set Initial Build Options) to Windows EXE, you can modify your program to look like Figure 2-4 (complete with window features and menus with underscores!). Try running the program by pressing ALT-R E within the PWB. Windows will start up automatically, and your program will run immediately.

Something new has also happened here. Windows programs must, of course, be run under the Windows environment. If you try to run one of these programs at the standard DOS prompt, you will see a message similar to this:

```
C:\> power
This program requires Microsoft Windows.
C:\>
```

This is the standard way to let your users know that Windows is required for the correct execution of your program. This output is printed

A simple FORTRAN program running in Windows

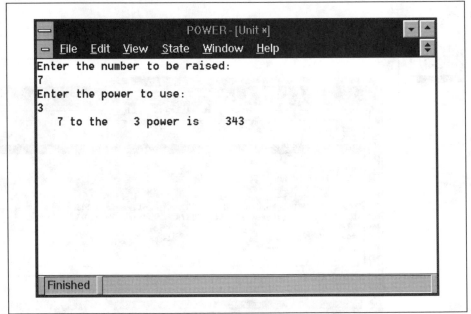

by a program called WINSTUB.EXE, which is found in your FORTRAN BINB directory. When you build Windows programs, the WINSTUB program is linked into your EXE file by default, causing the message to appear whenever an attempt is made to start the program outside of Windows. If you would like to write your own version of WINSTUB.EXE and place it in the FORTRAN BINB directory, you can create a more personalized message. For instance, the following code shows a simple replacement WINSTUB program that is personalized with the programmer's name.

```
$FREEFORM

"    Filename: WinStub.FOR

"    Replacement for the standard Windows stub. This one
"    has a nicer, personalized message.

"    By:       L. John Ribar
"    Date:     12 Sept 1994
"    System:   Microsoft FORTRAN 5.1
"    OS:       DOS

     Program WinStub

     Write(*,'(A)') ' This is a Windows program. Please run it'
     Write(*,'(A)') ' using Microsoft Windows.'
     Write(*,'(A)') ' Programmed by L. John Ribar, CCP'

     End
```

 Remember The WINSTUB program *must* be created as a DOS EXE file. If not, your message will not be displayed to the user; after all, this is a reminder that the program requires Windows!

If you were to copy the revised WINSTUB.EXE file into your FORTRAN BINB directory, your programs would have a message like this when run from the DOS command line:

```
C:\> power
This is a Windows program. Please run it
using Microsoft Windows.
Programmed by L. John Ribar, CCP
C:\>
```

The program in the preceding listing also illustrates the use of the **$FREEFORM** directive in a FORTRAN program. Using **$FREEFORM** allows you to relax the "Column 7 Rule" of standard FORTRAN. In fact, several of the rules change, as summarized here:

Coding Changes	Standard FORTRAN	$FREEFORM FORTRAN
Comments	C or asterisk (*) in column 1	Quotation marks (") start a comment if placed in column 1. An exclamation point (!) as the first non-blank character allows a comment to start anywhere on a line.
Continuation	Non-blank character in column 6	A hyphen (-) placed at the end of the line that needs to be continued.
Program lines	Always start at or after column 7	Can start in any column.
Statement labels	Columns 1 through 5	1- through 5-digit label as the first item found on the line.

While the switch to **$FREEFORM** may not seem to be an exciting change, it does allow for a more stylistic approach to programming. It also removes the requirement that specific columns be used for new lines. This flexibility is especially helpful with the PWB (and many other editors) that do not tab to column 7 by default. Another program using freeform formatting is shown here:

```
$FREEFORM

" Filename:    Average.FOR

" This is another example program that uses $FREEFORM formatting
" of code in a FORTRAN program. It averages a sequence of
" numbers given by the user.

" Author:   L. John Ribar
" Date:     13 Sept 1994
" System:   Microsoft FORTRAN 5.1
" OS:       DOS or Windows
```

```
      PROGRAM Average

"     List of numbers
      INTEGER*2   NumList(100)

"     Number of items entered
      INTEGER*2   ListCnt

"     Total amount of all items added together
      INTEGER*4   TotalCnt

"     Count Variables
      INTEGER*2   i, j

"     Initialize
      DATA   ListCnt /0/, TotalCnt/0/

      Write(*,*) ' AVERAGE - Average a sequence of numbers.'
      Write(*,*) ' Enter up to 100 numbers to be averaged.'
      Write(*,*) ' Use 0 as the last number.'

      DO i = 1,100
        Write(*,101) i
        Read(*,102) j
        IF (j .EQ. 0) THEN
           ListCnt = i-1
           GOTO 10
        ELSE
           NumList(i) = j
           TotalCnt = TotalCnt + j
        END IF
      END DO
10    CONTINUE

      Write(*,103) ListCnt, TotalCnt / ListCnt

101   FORMAT(' Please enter the next item (number ', -
       I2, '): ')
102   FORMAT(I4)
103   FORMAT(' The average value of the ', I3, ' entered is ' -
       I4, '.')

      END
```

You might notice many similarities to your existing code. Freeform formatting is not meant to be earthshaking; it just relaxes the rules a bit so you can spend more time programming and less time counting spaces. It is *optional*, so use whichever format you prefer.

Freeform formatting can be used in your programs by including the **$FREEFORM** statement in your program files, or by using the /4Yf option when compiling from the command line.

Using the information presented in the last example, try to compile the AVERAGE program for DOS and then for Windows. The output of the programs will be notably different—look at Figures 2-5 and 2-6.

Compiling from the Command Line

If you choose not to run the FORTRAN compiler from the Programmer's Workbench, you can run it from the DOS command line. This method is useful if you are using another editor, or if you simply like better control and visibility of everything that is happening.

To call the FORTRAN compiler, run the program FL.EXE from the DOS command line. The format of the command is as follows.

FL *options filenames*

FIGURE 2-5

The AVERAGE program in DOS

```
C:\BOOKS\4>Average
 AVERAGE - Average a sequence of numbers.
 Enter up to 100 numbers to be averaged.
 Use 0 as the last number.
Please enter the next item (number  1):
5
Please enter the next item (number  2):
10
Please enter the next item (number  3):
15
Please enter the next item (number  4):
20
Please enter the next item (number  5):
15
Please enter the next item (number  6):
0
The average value of the   5 entered is    13.

C:\BOOKS\4>
```

FIGURE
2-6

The AVERAGE program in Windows

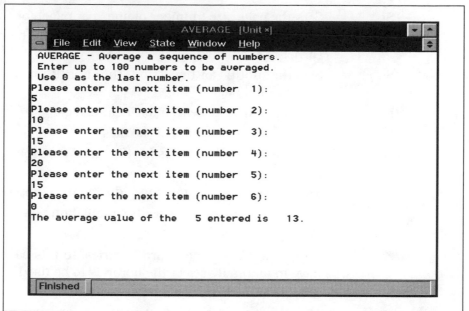

The list of possible options for FL is quite lengthy, and is covered in the FORTRAN Reference Manual supplied with the compiler. A few of the more important options that you'll want to remember are listed here:

Option	Purpose
/HELP	Displays help about the valid FL options. This actually calls the Microsoft QuickHelp program, a hypertext-based help system that helps you find the help you need quickly.
/c	Compiles, but does not link the files.
/Fo	Gives a specific name to the object file created.
/Fe	Gives a specific name to the executable file created. By default, the name of the first file being compiled will form the base of the executable program.
/Fs	Creates a source listing file.
/Fa	Creates an assembly code listing file.
/Fc	Creates a combined source and object listing file.
/Sl	Sets the line size (width) of the listing.

Option	Purpose
/Sp	Sets the page size (number of lines per page) for the listing.
/St	Sets the title for the listing. The title prints in the upper-left corner of each page.
/Ss	Sets the subtitle for the listing. The subtitle prints below the title on each page.
/I	Specifies where to search for Include files.
/Zs	Only checks the syntax of the files.
/Zi	Prepares the file for use with the Microsoft CodeView debugger.
/W0	Suppresses warning messages during the compilation.
/Od	Removes optimization; speeds compilation.
/Ox	Full optimization.
/Zl	Suppresses use of standard libraries. In this case, you will have to manually select the libraries to be used.
/F	Sets the size of the stack.
/V	Places a string (label) into the OBJ file. This is often used to embed a version number or copyright notice into the final program.
/MW	Creates a Windows program using the QuickWin library.
/4Ys	Enables all Microsoft extensions (default).
/4YV	Enables only IBM VS extensions.
/4Yv	Enables only VAX extensions.
/4Yi	Enables only SAA extensions.
/4Yf	Enables freeform format.
/4Nf	Disables freeform format (default).

If you wanted to compile the AVERAGE program for use under Windows, creating a source listing file with "Average Program" as the title and the programmer's name as the subtitle, you would use the following command line:

```
FL Average.FOR /Fs /St"Average Program" /Ss"L.J. Ribar" /MW
```

Once you determine the options you will use most often, you can use the FL environment variable to save them and apply them to all your compilations. For instance, to create Windows programs, along with source listings that are ready for debugging with CodeView, you might put the following command in your AUTOEXEC.BAT file:

```
SET FL=/Zi /MW /Fs
```

Using VAX and IBM Extensions

To help in porting (converting) your existing FORTRAN programs to the PC, Microsoft has added both IBM and VAX extensions to their compiler. These extensions are enabled by default as part of the Microsoft extensions. However, you can specify that you want only specific extensions enabled by using the compiler option /4Yv (enable only VAX extensions) or /4YV (enable only IBM VS extensions). In either case, Microsoft becomes a strict FORTRAN-77 compiler, adding only the extensions selected (VAX or IBM). In this way, the Microsoft compiler can be used for IBM or VAX development.

These capabilities can be enabled within the PWB by using the Options menu (ALT-O for Options, and F for FORTRAN Compiler Options), as shown in Figure 2-7.

For more complete information on these options, be sure to look into the Microsoft FORTRAN Reference and Advanced Topics manuals.

IBM VS Extensions

The following options are available in IBM VS-compatibility mode.

Variable names of 31 characters are allowed. This is in contrast to the FORTRAN standard of allowing only six characters to be significant (meaning that the compiler calls variable names longer than six characters by only the first six characters). Microsoft FORTRAN normally allows longer variable names, but this option is specifically designed for IBM VS compatibility.

Integer arrays are allowed to contain **FORMAT** specifications.

The **DO-WHILE** statement allows sections of code to be processed repeatedly until a specific condition becomes true. This enhances the

FIGURE
2-7

Selecting compilation options in the PWB

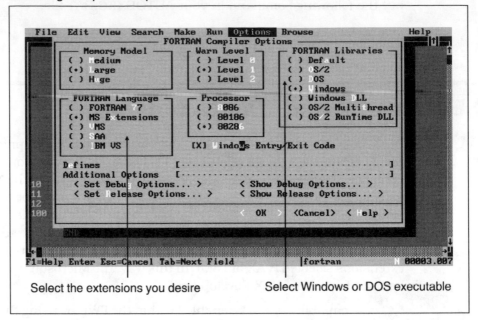

Select the extensions you desire   Select Windows or DOS executable

readability (and reduces the complexity) of FORTRAN programs. For instance, you can now end a loop early by setting the loop variable beyond the upper bound that is being checked, *without* using a **GOTO** statement! The following three pieces of code, therefore, perform equivalent functions:

```
C       An older looping structure
        I = 1
10      CONTINUE
          WRITE(*,*) I
          I = I + 1
C       The only way out of this loop is with a GOTO
        IF (I.GT.10) GOTO 20
        GOTO 10
20      CONTINUE

C       Looping using a DO loop
        DO 50, I=0,10
          WRITE(*,*) I
C         No need to increment I in this type of loop, but
```

```
C        what happens if you are done when I gets to 6 (for
C        some reason). Then, you need a GOTO to get out of
C        here!
         IF (I.GT.6) GOTO 60
50       CONTINUE

C        The next statement is the destination for the GOTO
C        statement shown above.
60       CONTINUE

C        Newer loop, using DO WHILE. Notice that no
C        GOTO statement is required, better supporting
C        structured programming concepts.
         I = 1
         DO WHILE (I.LE.10)
           WRITE(*,*) I
           I = I + 1
C          If you need to get out after 6, just set the
C          looping variable greater than the loop bounds.
           IF (I.GT.6) I = 11
         END DO
```

DO statements can be used without specified labels. This provides for a cleaner, more modern structured look; one of the most confusing requirements of older FORTRAN compilers was that every **DO** loop required a labeled statement at the end of the loop. As an example, look at the two **DO** loops in the next listing:

```
C     An older DO loop
      DO 10, I=0,10
      DO 20, J=1,5
      WRITE(*,*) I, J
20    CONTINUE
10    CONTINUE

C     A newer style
      DO I=0,10
        DO J=1,5
          WRITE(*,*) I, J
        END DO
      END DO
```

This listing also shows the use of the **END DO** statement ending a **DO** loop or a **DO-WHILE** loop when a labeled statement is not used.

EQUIVALENCE can be used to equate character and non-character items. Previously, an **EQUIVALENCE** could only be used with two character items, or with two non-character items. Now, character and non-character items can be equivalent. One restriction, however, is that the non-character item must start on an even-byte boundary.

NAMELISTs can be declared and used with input and output. A declaration of a **NAMELIST** looks similar to a **DATA** or **COMMON** statement:

```
NAMELIST / namelist / variables
```

In this statement, **NAMELIST** is a keyword (like **DATA** or **COMMON**) that specifies what is being declared, *namelist* is the name of the **NAMELIST** being created, and *variables* is a list of the variable names being included. For instance, the following program

```
PROGRAM NameList

INTEGER*2    Age, Weight
CHARACTER    Name*15
REAL*4       Salary

NAMELIST /Person/ Age, Weight, Name, Salary

Age = 31
Weight = 205
Name = 'Fred Fredson'
Salary = 25125.25

WRITE(*, Person)

END
```

produces the following display of data if compiled for DOS:

```
&PERSON
AGE =              31
WEIGHT =             205
NAME = 'Fred Fredson    '
SALARY =     25125.250000
/
```

If compiled for Windows, the program produces the output shown in Figure 2-8.

FIGURE
2-8

NAMELIST output in Windows

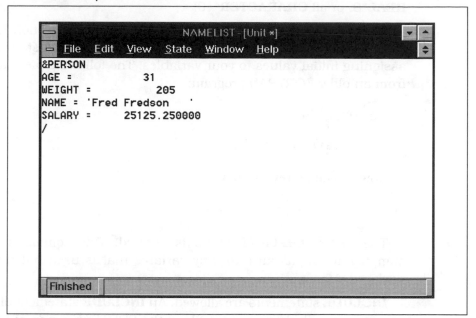

```
                        NAMELIST - [Unit *]
   File   Edit   View   State   Window   Help
&PERSON
AGE =              31
WEIGHT =                205
NAME = 'Fred Fredson        '
SALARY =      25125.250000
/




 Finished
```

Using **NAMELIST**s is an effective method for manipulating blocks of data. In fact, this method is especially handy when reading and writing data within files where you wish to specify only certain fields, and where the field names can be specified along with the data. An input file for **NAMELIST** processing would look similar to the output produced in the preceding example showing the **WRITE** statement. It would begin with the name of the list (&PERSON), followed by a list of fields, each with a field name (such as AGE =) and associated data (31 in the preceding case). Not all fields need to be given, and no specific order is required. The final line would consist of only a slash character (/).

The initialization of **COMMON** block data can be performed in **DATA** statements outside of **BLOCK DATA** subprograms. Normally, FORTRAN requires that initialization of **COMMON** blocks be done with **DATA** statements in a **BLOCK DATA** subprogram. This restriction has been relaxed in Microsoft FORTRAN.

The mixing of character and non-character items in **COMMON** areas is allowed. Many other versions of FORTRAN require that **COMMON** areas contain only variables of a common size (for example, all **INTEGER***2, all **REAL***8, or all **CHARACTER***10).

Initialization of variables can be done on the declaration line. This relieves you from using separate declaration and **DATA** statements for assigning initial values to your variables. The following piece of code is from an older FORTRAN program:

```
INTEGER*2   Age, Weight

DATA Age /31/, Weight /205/
```

Now, it can be rewritten as

```
INTEGER*2   Age /31/, Weight /205/
```

The use of **IMPLICIT NONE** is allowed. This command tells the compiler to flag as an error any variable that is used but that is not declared.

INCLUDE statements are allowed. An **INCLUDE** statement directs the compiler to include an outside file in the FORTRAN program file, at the point(s) specified, during compilation. An **INCLUDE** statement is often used with declarations of shared variables and **COMMON** areas, so that the definition does not need to be maintained in multiple locations, as you will see in the next two program listings. Shown here is the main program file:

```
$FREEFORM

"   Include.FOR

"   A program that shows the INCLUDE directive in use.
"   Author:    L. John Ribar
"   Date:      11 Sept 1994
"   System:    MS FORTRAN 5.1
"   OS:        DOS or Windows

    PROGRAM Include

    IMPLICIT NONE
    INCLUDE 'DataForm.INC'

"   First, set up the values
```

```
      LoanAmount = 80000.0
      BasePct = 10.5
      NumYears = 15.5

      CALL CalcPmt

      END



      SUBROUTINE CalcPmt

      IMPLICIT NONE
      INTEGER*2   I            ! Loop variable
      REAL*4      AmtLeft       ! Amount yet to be paid
      REAL*4      Principal     ! Annual principal amount
      REAL*4      Interest      ! Annual interest

      INCLUDE 'DataForm.INC'

      WRITE(*,100) LoanAmount, BasePct
      WRITE(*,110) NumYears
      AmtLeft = LoanAmount
      Principal = LoanAmount / NumYears    ! Annual Principal

"     Here is where you would put the actual calculations
      DO I=1,NumYears
          Interest = AmtLeft * (BasePct/100.0)
          AmtLeft = AmtLeft - Principal
          WRITE(*,10) I, Principal, Interest, Principal + Interest,-
              AmtLeft
      END DO

10    FORMAT(' ', I2, ': Prin ',F8.2,' Int ',F8.2, ' Payment ', -
          F12.2, '. Balance ',F12.2)
100   FORMAT(' Amount of loan: ',F12.2,'  Percentage Rate: ',F6.2)
110   FORMAT(' Term in years:  ',F4.1)

      END
```

This is the Include file, DATAFORM.INC:

```
"   DataForm.INC

    REAL*4      BasePct, NumYears, LoanAmount

    COMMON /LInfo/ BasePct, NumYears, LoanAmount
```

Another use for Include files is with declarations of external library routines. You'll see this procedure when you start using the QuickWin libraries for creating Windows-specific programs in Chapter 3, and when you are introduced to Windows API functions in Chapter 4.

Non-integer array subscripts are allowed. In standard FORTRAN programming, the use of a floating-point number as an array index would cause the number to be truncated, and the integer value generated would be used as the index. However, Microsoft allows the use of floating-point index values.

The Z descriptor is allowed in **FORMAT** statements. This descriptor is used to designate hexadecimal numbers.

Comment lines can start with exclamation points (!). In addition, a comment can be inserted at the end of a line of code by starting the comment with an exclamation point. Comments can be seen in several of the listings in this chapter.

The characters $ and _ may be used in naming identifiers. However, the underscore cannot be used as the first character of the name.

If you need to use these capabilities in your programs, especially if you are converting your programs from the IBM VS environment, they are available by default as part of the Microsoft FORTRAN extensions. If you want to disable the other Microsoft extensions, be sure to use the /4YV option when you compile from the command line. Within the PWB, set the option in the FORTRAN Compiler Options screen (which was shown in Figure 2-7).

VAX Extensions

The following options are available in the VAX compatibility mode.

Variable names of 31 characters are allowed. This is in contrast to the FORTRAN standard of allowing only six characters to be significant (meaning that the compiler calls variable names longer than six characters by only the first six characters). Microsoft FORTRAN normally allows longer variable names, but this option is also included as part of VAX compatibility.

Integer arrays may contain **FORMAT** statements.

Debugging comment lines are allowed. Comment lines that begin with D in column 1 are included in the compilation if Debug mode is specified, but remain as comments at all other times. This is often used for **WRITE** statements during the debugging phase of a program's development.

The **DO-WHILE** statement allows sections of code to be processed repeatedly until a specific condition becomes true. This enhances the readability (and reduces the complexity) of FORTRAN programs. For instance, you can now end a loop early by setting the loop variable beyond the upper bound that is being checked, *without* using a **GOTO** statement! The following three pieces of code, therefore, perform equivalent functions:

```
C      An older looping structure
       I = 1
10     CONTINUE
         WRITE(*,*) I
         I = I + 1
C        The only way out of this loop is with a GOTO
         IF (I.GT.10) GOTO 20
         GOTO 10
20     CONTINUE


C      Looping using a DO loop
       DO 50, I=0,10
         WRITE(*,*) I
C        No need to increment I in this type of loop, but
C        what happens if you are done when I gets to 6 (for
C        some reason). Then, you need a GOTO to get out of
C        here!
         IF (I.GT.6) GOTO 60
50     CONTINUE


C      The next statement is the destination for the GOTO
C      statement shown above.
60     CONTINUE


C      Newer loop, using DO WHILE. Notice that no
C      GOTO statement is required, better supporting
C      structured programming concepts.
       I = 1
       DO WHILE (I.LE.10)
         WRITE(*,*) I
         I = I + 1
C        If you need to get out after 6, just set the
```

```
C       looping variable greater than the loop bounds.
        IF (I.GT.6) I = 11
      END DO
```

DO statements can be used without specified labels. This provides for a cleaner, more modern structured look; one of the most confusing requirements of older FORTRAN compilers was that every **DO** loop required a labeled statement at the end of the loop. As an example, look at the two **DO** loops in the next listing:

```
C      An older DO loop
       DO 10, I=0,10
       DO 20, J=1,5
       WRITE(*,*) I, J
20     CONTINUE
10     CONTINUE

C      A newer style
       DO I=0,10
         DO J=1,5
           WRITE(*,*) I, J
         END DO
       END DO
```

This listing also shows the use of the **END DO** statement for ending a **DO** loop or a **DO-WHILE** loop when a labeled statement is not used.

EQUIVALENCE can be used to equate character and non-character items. Previously, an **EQUIVALENCE** could only be used with two character items, or with two non-character items. Now, character and non-character items can be equivalent. One restriction, however, is that the non-character item must start on an even-byte boundary.

An **EQUIVALENCE** with multidimensional arrays can be performed with a single subscript.

REAL and **COMPLEX** data types can use exponentiation. (Up until now, the use of exponentiation has been restricted to integer numbers.)

The use of **IMPLICIT NONE** is allowed. This command tells the compiler to flag any variable as an error that is used but that is not declared.

INCLUDE statements are allowed. An **INCLUDE** statement directs the compiler to include an outside file in the FORTRAN program file, at the point(s) specified, during compilation. An **INCLUDE** statement is often used with declarations of shared variables and **COMMON** areas, so that the definition does not need to be maintained in multiple locations, as shown in the next two program listings. Here is the main program file:

```
$FREEFORM

"    Include.FOR

"    A program that shows the INCLUDE directive in use.
"    Author:      L. John Ribar
"    Date:        11 Sept 1994
"    System:      MS FORTRAN 5.1
"    OS:          DOS or Windows

     PROGRAM Include

     IMPLICIT NONE
     INCLUDE 'DataForm.INC'

"    First, set up the values
     LoanAmount = 80000.0
     BasePct = 10.5
     NumYears = 15.5

     CALL CalcPmt

     END



     SUBROUTINE CalcPmt

     IMPLICIT NONE
     INTEGER*2   I            ! Loop variable
     REAL*4      AmtLeft       ! Amount yet to be paid
     REAL*4      Principal     ! Annual principal amount
     REAL*4      Interest      ! Annual interest

     INCLUDE 'DataForm.INC'

     WRITE(*,100) LoanAmount, BasePct
     WRITE(*,110) NumYears
     AmtLeft = LoanAmount
```

```
        Principal = LoanAmount / NumYears   ! Annual Principal

"     Here is where you would put the actual calculations
      DO I=1,NumYears
          Interest = AmtLeft * (BasePct/100.0)
          AmtLeft = AmtLeft - Principal
          WRITE(*,10) I, Principal, Interest, Principal + Interest-
              AmtLeft
      END DO

10    FORMAT(' ', I2, ': Prin ',F8.2,' Int ',F8.2, ' Payment ', -
          F12.2, '. Balance ',F12.2)
100   FORMAT(' Amount of loan: ',F12.2,'  Percentage Rate: ',F6.2)
110   FORMAT(' Term in years:  ',F4.1)

      END
```

This is the Include file, DATAFORM.INC:

```
"    DataForm.INC

     REAL*4       BasePct, NumYears, LoanAmount

     COMMON /LInfo/ BasePct, NumYears, LoanAmount
```

 Note   Include files can also be used with declarations of external library routines. You'll see this procedure when you start using the QuickWin libraries for creating Windows-specific programs in Chapter 3, and when you are introduced to Windows API functions in Chapter 4.

Initialization of variables can be done on the declaration line. This relieves you from using separate declaration and **DATA** statements for assigning initial values to your variables. The following piece of code is from an older FORTRAN program:

```
INTEGER*2   Age, Weight

DATA Age /31/, Weight /205/
```

Now, it can be rewritten as

```
INTEGER*2   Age /31/, Weight /205/
```

Non-integer array subscripts are allowed. In standard FORTRAN programming, the use of a floating-point number as an array index would cause the number to be truncated, and the integer value generated would be used as the index. However, Microsoft allows the use of floating-point index values.

The initialization of **COMMON** block data can be performed in **DATA** statements outside of **BLOCK DATA** subprograms. Traditionally, FORTRAN requires that initialization of **COMMON** blocks can only be done with **DATA** statements in a **BLOCK DATA** subprogram. This restriction has been relaxed in Microsoft FORTRAN.

The mixing of character and non-character items in **COMMON** areas is allowed. Many other implementations of FORTRAN require that **COMMON** areas must contain only variables of a common size (for example, all **INTEGER***2, all **REAL***8, or all **CHARACTER***10).

The **STRUCTURE**, **UNION**, and **MAP** statements are allowed.

Up to 99 continuation lines are allowed for a statement.

The dollar sign ($) can be used in identifiers.

The .XOR. operator can be used in logical comparisons. The XOR operation provides a TRUE value if one of the operands, but not both, is TRUE. In all other cases, the output is FALSE. This table summarizes the outputs:

Op1	Op2	Op1 .XOR. Op2
.TRUE.	.TRUE.	.FALSE.
.TRUE.	.FALSE.	.TRUE.
.FALSE.	.TRUE.	.TRUE.
.FALSE.	.FALSE.	.FALSE.

The keywords **APPEND**, **BLOCKSIZE**, and **NML** can be used with input and output:

☐ With an **OPEN** statement, the **ACCESS=APPEND** specifier positions the file pointer to the end of the file, ready for new information to be appended to the end of the file. By default, **OPEN** positions the file pointer at the beginning of the file, so any **WRITE** statements overwrite some of the information stored at the beginning of the file.

☐ The **BLOCKSIZE=** parameter to **OPEN** specifies the size of the internal buffer used for reading and writing data. **BLOCK SIZE=** is often used to reduce the number of times that the file must be physically read; data can instead be read as needed from the buffer. The buffer is handled internally by the FORTRAN library functions. The default buffer size is 2048 bytes.

☐ The **NML=** parameter to a **WRITE** or **READ** statement allows the use of **NAMELIST**s in FORTRAN programs. **NML=** is optional, and used only when other parameters (such as **END=**) are used in the **WRITE** or **READ** statement.

Declaration of a **NAMELIST** looks similar to a **DATA** or **COMMON** statement:

```
NAMELIST / namelist / variables
```

NAMELIST is a keyword (like **DATA** or **COMMON**) that specifies what is being declared, *namelist* is the name of the **NAMELIST** being created, and *variables* is a list of the variable names being included. For instance, the following program

```
        PROGRAM NameList

        INTEGER*2    Age, Weight
        CHARACTER    Name*15
        REAL*4       Salary

        NAMELIST /Person/ Age, Weight, Name, Salary

        Age = 31
        Weight = 205
        Name = 'Fred Fredson'
        Salary = 25125.25

        WRITE(*, Person)
C       Could also be written as
C       WRITE(*, NML=Person)

        END
```

produces the following display of data if compiled for DOS:

```
&PERSON
AGE =              31
WEIGHT =               205
NAME = 'Fred Fredson       '
SALARY =        25125.250000
/
```

If compiled for Windows, the program produces the output shown in Figure 2-8.

Using **NAMELIST**s is an effective method for manipulating blocks of data. In fact, this method is especially handy when reading and writing data within files where you only wish to specify certain fields, and where the field names can be specified along with the data. An input file for **NAMELIST** processing would look similar to the output produced in the preceding example showing the **WRITE** statement. It would begin with the name of the list (&PERSON), followed by a list of fields, each with a field name (such as AGE =) and associated data (31 in the preceding case). Not all fields need to be given, and no specific order is required. The final line would consist of only a slash character (/).

Logical operations (.AND., .OR., and so on) can use numeric operands. In most FORTRAN implementations, this is not true; only logical variables or expressions can be used. Microsoft FORTRAN allows the use of integer variables, producing an integer result, resulting from the bitwise manipulation of the operands. For instance, after the following piece of code executes, the variable *I* will contain the value 3.

```
      I = 1 .OR. 2

C     1 is binary 0001, 2 is binary 0010.
C     Therefore, 1 .OR. 2 results in binary 0011.
C     With the OR operation, for each bit, if a 1
C     appears in either operand, it will also appear
C     in the final value.
```

If you need to use these capabilities in your programs, especially if you are converting your programs from the VAX environment, they are available by default as part of the Microsoft FORTRAN extensions. If you want to disable the other Microsoft extensions, be sure to use the /4Yv option when you compile from the command line. Within the PWB, set the option in the FORTRAN Compiler Options screen (which was shown in Figure 2-7).

Using the QuickWin Libraries

The QuickWin libraries supplied with the Microsoft FORTRAN compiler allow standard FORTRAN programs to be recompiled for Windows without any major changes.

In Chapter 3, you'll see how easy it is to write Windows programs in FORTRAN using the QuickWin libraries. Then, in Chapter 4, you'll learn how the WATCOM FORTRAN compiler lets you bring your code into Windows.

CHAPTER

Writing Real
Windows Programs in
Microsoft FORTRAN

*I*n Chapter 2, you saw how easily a Windows program can be created by just recompiling your existing FORTRAN code. This is possible because of the text-based QuickWin libraries found in Microsoft FORTRAN. In this chapter, you'll learn how to add Windows-specific extensions to your programs.

There are two separate Microsoft FORTRAN libraries available for adding Windows capabilities to your FORTRAN programs. One is the standard QuickWin library, used for text programming. The other is the QuickWin Graphics library, which allows the addition of graphics to your programs. The Microsoft FORTRAN installation book instructs you in the building of these libraries. Once they are built, you are ready to create Windows programs. The next sections will cover the use of these libraries in more detail.

The QuickWin Text Library

The FORTRAN QuickWin library is linked into your programs automatically when you use the /MW option from the command line, or when you select Windows EXE in the Build options from the PWB. This library allows standard FORTRAN programs to run under Windows, each in its own window. As in other Windows applications, the windows used for your FORTRAN programs can be sized, reduced to icons, maximized to full-screen size, and moved. In addition, a fixed menu bar is provided automatically for all QuickWin programs; Figure 3-1 depicts this standard menu bar.

While this environment is not really exciting in terms of Windows programs, it provides you with the ability to run your existing FORTRAN programs under a graphical user interface without changing a single line of code!

The QuickWin program that displays the window shown in Figure 3-1 is shown here:

```
$FREEFORM

"    SimplWin.FOR
"    An extremely simple FORTRAN program for Windows.
"    Author:    L. John Ribar
```

```
"    Date:         11 Sept 1994
"    System:       MS FORTRAN 5.1
"    OS:           MS Windows

     PROGRAM SimplWin

"    You don't really need any code here!  But to keep it
"    lively, say hello to the user.
     WRITE (*,*) 'Hello, user!'

     END
```

The program is compiled from the command line using the following command:

```
FL /MW SimplWin.FOR
```

Now that you have seen the development of a complete Windows program (albeit a simple one) under FORTRAN, you might want to know

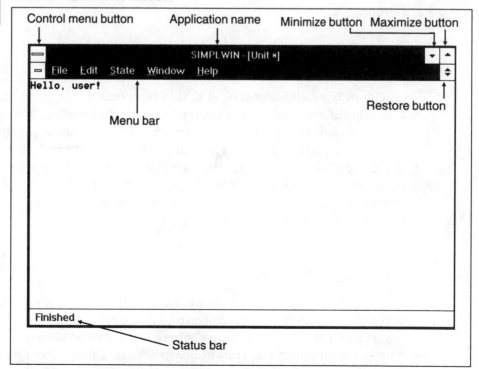

FIGURE 3-1

A default QuickWin window

Control menu button   Application name   Minimize button   Maximize button

SIMPLWIN - [Unit ×]

File   Edit   State   Window   Help

Hello, user!

Restore button

Menu bar

Finished

Status bar

what features the default QuickWin window provides. Then you'll learn how to enhance your programs to make use of Windows-specific features.

The Default QuickWin Window

The default window provided by QuickWin is shown in Figure 3-1. The menu bar across the top of the window includes the following menu entries: File, Edit, State, Window, and Help. The following sections discuss each of these menus.

You may also notice when you create your first QuickWin programs that all the text displayed by the programs uses black text on a white background. This is the default for all QuickWin applications.

The File Menu

The File menu in a QuickWin program has only one option, shown here:

The only available option is Exit, which causes the program to exit. You should also notice the CTRL-C next to the Exit option. This is known as an *accelerator key*. An accelerator key can be pressed at any time while the program is running, even if the menus are not currently selected, and the option associated with that accelerator key will be executed. For instance, you can press CTRL-C (press CTRL and hold it down while pressing C) at any time while a QuickWin program is running, and the program will immediately stop.

The Edit Menu

The Edit menu is used to interact with other Windows programs through a facility called the clipboard. The *clipboard* is an area of memory, reserved for Windows programs, where items can be placed for transferring between programs. The clipboard acts very much like its real-world counterpart—items can be clipped onto the clipboard by one program, and can be clipped off of the clipboard by another (or the same) program. The Edit menu is shown here:

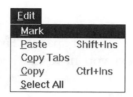

Mark   The Mark option of the Edit menu allows a portion of the window to be marked for placement onto the clipboard. When Mark is selected, you will see a vertical-bar cursor appear in the upper-left corner of the window. Simply move the bar, using the arrow keys or the mouse, to the place where you want to start marking the text. Then, hold the SHIFT key down and move to the end of the area you'd like marked. As you move the bar, the marked text will be highlighted (shown in a reverse color) so you can tell where you've been. Finally, press CTRL-INS to copy the text to the clipboard.

While you are marking text to be copied to the clipboard, the program is paused (it stops running temporarily). Pausing your QuickWin programs is discussed in the State Menu section later in this chapter.

Once you have marked the text and copied it to the clipboard, you can use it in any other Windows program that supports the clipboard; simply select the Paste option within that program.

Text can also be copied with the mouse. Point at the top-left corner of the area you wish to mark. Press and hold down the left mouse button, and drag the pointer to the end of the area you wish to mark. Then release the left button and select Copy Tabs or Copy from the Edit menu.

Paste   The Paste option of the Edit menu allows you to retrieve information from the clipboard (whether it was placed there from the current program or from another program). If another program has placed information onto the clipboard, choosing Paste in your program will retrieve that information, allowing it to be used as input for your current program. The accelerator key for Paste is SHIFT-INS.

Copy Tabs The Copy Tabs option copies the highlighted text to the clipboard, adding tabs at any place where one or more spaces occur. This is useful for some programs, like Microsoft Excel, that use tab characters to parse data.

Copy The Copy option copies the highlighted text to the clipboard, but does not substitute tabs for spaces. The text placed on the clipboard looks exactly like the text you have marked. the accelerator key for Copy is CTRL-INS.

Select All The Select All option selects and highlights the text in the current window. Once this is done, you can use Copy or Copy Tabs to move the information to the clipboard.

The State Menu

The State menu, shown here, is used to pause and restart your QuickWin programs. The Pause option is useful when you are going to use the Edit menu options, or when you want to stop the program for any other reason.

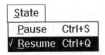

Select the Pause option to temporarily stop execution of your program. The accelerator key for this option is CTRL-S. The Resume option will restart your program from the point at which it was paused. The accelerator key for Resume is CTRL-Q.

The Window Menu

The following shows the standard Window menu in a QuickWin program:

The options described next are available from the Window menu.

Cascade   The Cascade option rearranges all the child windows within your application's window so that they are stacked, showing only the top line (the title bar) of each window. This is the default method of displaying child windows. (You'll learn more about creating child windows in the next few sections.) Figure 3-2 shows an example of the cascade layout.

Cascaded windows in standard FORTRAN

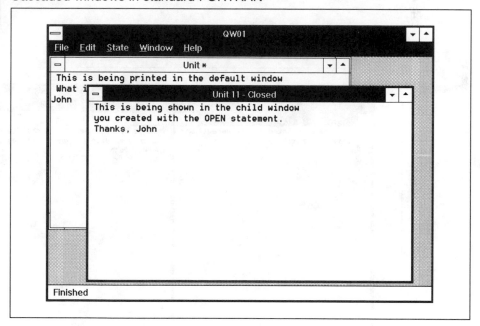

Tile The Tile option rearranges the child windows of your application so that they are all uncovered and are displayed next to each other. An example of the tiled arrangement is shown in Figure 3-3.

Arrange Icons One capability available to your child windows is that they can be *minimized,* or *iconized.* while your application is active. To minimize a window, click on its Minimize button (the downward-pointing arrowhead button at the upper right). Once minimized, your windows appear as icons, which are small drawings representing each window. The Arrange Icons option of the Window menu arranges the icons neatly within your application window. Figure 3-4 shows a set of child windows reduced to icons. To restore a window to its previous status, double-click on its icon.

Input The Input option is available only when your application is awaiting input from the user. In this case, the Input option moves the focus to the window awaiting input, so that the user can enter data. *Focus* pertains to which window should have the current attention of the user.

FIGURE
3-3

Tiling the windows for better viewing

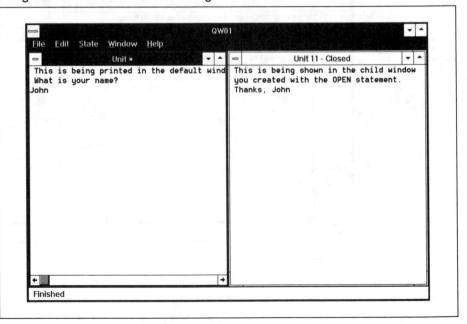

FIGURE
3-4

Child windows minimized to icons

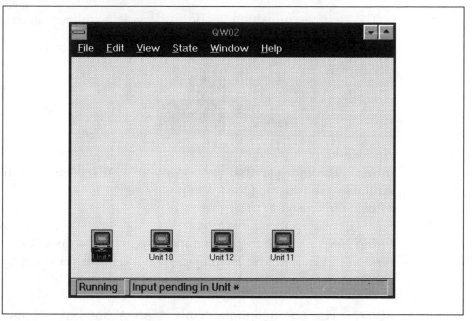

The window that has the focus is denoted with a highlighted window title bar, so that you can quickly find it.

Clear Paste   The Clear Paste option empties the clipboard. The clipboard is filled using options from the Edit menu (discussed above).

Status Bar   The Status Bar command turns the status bar on and off. The status bar is located at the bottom of your application's window. It is used to present messages from the QuickWin library, telling you, for instance, when input is required in a particular child window.

Other Options   Beneath the options listed so far, there will be a list by name, of the currently available windows. The window that currently has the focus will be marked with a check mark. If you want to move the focus to another window, select that window from the menu, either with the mouse or by typing the number to the left of it when the menu is displayed.

The Help Menu

The Help menu, which is shown here, lets you access the QuickWin Help library. There are three options available.

Index   The Index option presents you with the index of information available about using QuickWin programs. This Help library is provided with the Microsoft FORTRAN compiler.

Using Help   The Using Help option instructs you how to use the Help system in general. The Help system is a feature provided by Microsoft Windows.

About   The About option displays an About box. About boxes are generally used to display the program's name, version, and often the programmer's name. Later in this chapter, you will see how to create your own About boxes.

Recompiling Your Existing Programs

Here is a program written in FORTRAN for Microsoft Windows. In this program you will see a request for information from the user, and display of an answer. One difference you'll notice from other FORTRAN programs is that the FILE used in the **OPEN** statement is specified as 'USER'; this will add a child window to the program. By using this method in your programs, you provide separate windows for input and output.

```
C    QW01.FOR
C    FORTRAN Program for Windows. This program just
C    opens as a Windows program, adds a child window,
C    and then quits.
C
C    Author:    L. John Ribar
C    Date:      11 Sept 1994
```

```
C      System:     MS FORTRAN 5.1
C      OS:         MS Windows
C

       Program QW01

       CHARACTER*20 Name

C      Add a child window.
       OPEN( UNIT=11, FILE='USER' )

       WRITE( *,* ) ' This is being printed in the default
     +  window'
       WRITE( *,* ) ' What is your name? '
       READ(  *, '(A)' ) Name

       WRITE(11,* ) ' This is being shown in the child window'
       WRITE(11,* ) ' you created with the OPEN statement.'
       WRITE(11,* ) ' Thanks, ', Name


       END
```

This program can be compiled for Windows by use of the following command:

```
FL /MW QW01.FOR
```

To see the result of running the child window program under Windows, review Figure 3-2.

The only big problem you might notice is that when information is displayed in the child window, it covers the default window. One way to see both windows is to use the Window menu's Tile option, which will give you a screen that looks like Figure 3-3. To do this from within your program, you'll need to add Windows-specific code, which will be covered in the next section.

There is still more you can do with your windows, however. You may wish to add a title to each window so the user knows what to expect there. This is accomplished using the **TITLE=** directive in the **OPEN** statement, as done in the next listing.

```
C      QW01N.FOR
C      FORTRAN Program for Windows. This program just
```

```
C       opens as a Windows program, adds a child window,
C       along with a title, and then quits.
C
C       Author:    L. John Ribar
C       Date:      11 Sept 1994
C       System:    MS FORTRAN 5.1
C       OS:        MS Windows
C

        Program QW01N

        CHARACTER*20 Name

C       Add a named child window.
        OPEN( UNIT=11, FILE='USER', TITLE='My Child Win' )

        WRITE( *,* ) ' This is being printed in the default
     +  window'
        WRITE( *,* ) ' What is your name? '
        READ(   *, '(A)' ) Name

        WRITE(11,* ) ' This is being shown in the child window'
        WRITE(11,* ) ' you created with the OPEN statement.'
        WRITE(11,* ) ' Thanks, ', Name

        END
```

As you can see in Figure 3-5, assigning titles makes your program easier to use; leaving the windows titled only by their Unit number is very confusing to a user.

To aid the user of your application in determining the next thing to be done, the focus of a window can be set when that window is used for input or output. This is done by adding the following parameter to your **OPEN** statement:

```
IOFOCUS = .TRUE.
```

This causes the window to receive the focus (and causes its title bar to change color) when the window is being used for input or output. The default setting of **IOFOCUS=** is FALSE, meaning that the user will see information being displayed in different windows, but that there will be no change in which window has the current focus.

FIGURE 3-5

Adding window titles for better understanding

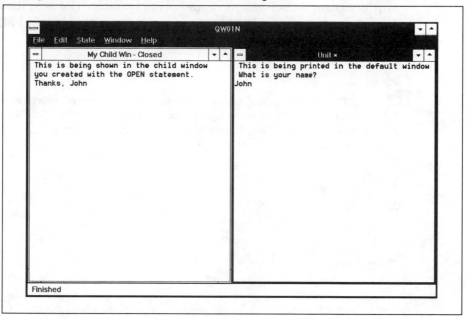

Adding Windows-Specific Code

Windows-specific coding in FORTRAN requires knowledge of the Windows programming environment and nonstandard FORTRAN routines, as provided by QuickWin. To use these routines, you must link your programs using the /MW compiler option. In addition, the files FLIB.FI and FLIB.FD must be included in your program file.

Using FI and FD Files

Interface (FI) and Declaration (FD) files are supplied by Microsoft for use with the QuickWin libraries. FI files contain function and subroutine declarations for routines included in the libraries. FD files contain structure and constant declarations, which enhance the readability of your programs.

FLIB.FI is an interface file that contains descriptions of the functions and subroutines used to access the QuickWin Windows-specific features.

Because this file contains interface information, it must be included in your program file before any actual program code. The next listing shows the correct location of **INCLUDE** statements for both FI and FD files.

```
      INCLUDE 'FLIB.FI'                  ! Interface routines

C     QW02.FOR
C     FORTRAN Program for Windows. This program starts up
C     under Windows, and opens some child windows. The windows
C     are tiled. Then, some messages are displayed before
C     exiting.
C
C     Author:    L. John Ribar
C     Date:      11 Sept 1994
C     System:    MS FORTRAN 5.1
C     OS:        MS Windows

      Program QW02

      INCLUDE 'FLIB.FD'                  ! Definitions
      INTEGER*2   I                      ! Counting/Status
      INTEGER*2   W                      ! Window number

      OPEN( UNIT=10, FILE='USER')        ! Open the first child
      OPEN( UNIT=11, FILE='USER')        ! Open the second child
      OPEN( UNIT=12, FILE='USER')        ! Open the third child

C     Now, simulate the Window Tile menu command
      I = CLICKQQ( QWIN$TILE )

C     Now, write to the windows. Notice that the default
C     window (with highlighted title) does not change as the
C     text is written into each window.

      W = 10
      DO WHILE (W .NE. 0)
          WRITE(*,*) ' Pick a window (10,11,12 or 0 to quit): '
          READ(*,'(I2)') W
          IF ( (W.LT.10).OR.(W.GT.12)) GOTO 200

          WRITE( W, * ) 'Writing to your window now!'
200   END DO

      END                                ! End of program
```

FLIB.FD contains the structures used by the Windows interface routines. In addition, symbolic constants (such as QWIN$TILE in the listing above) are declared. These symbolic references make reading your program a much simpler task.

Now that the interface and definition files have been included in your program file, you are ready to use the Windows-specific routines in your applications.

Functions for Manipulating Windows

One of the first things you might want to do with a Windows program is to modify how a window appears to the application's user. There are several QuickWin routines to help you accomplish this.

In the earlier sections of this chapter, you saw how to open a child window (using **OPEN**), add a title to that window (with **TITLE=** in the **OPEN** statement), and control whether the window would have focus when input and output occurred (using **IOFOCUS=** in the **OPEN** statement). Now you need to learn how to manipulate the size and position of the windows themselves.

The simplest way to display all the child windows in your application at once is to let Windows tile them. This can be done by the user (with the Window menu's Tile option), but it will be easier if the tiling is done automatically by your program.

The CLICKQQ function is used to simulate mouse clicks on the menus. This function was used in the previous listing to simulate the Window menu's Tile option illustrated in Figure 3-4. The interface to this function, as found in FLIB.FI, is shown here:

```
INTERFACE TO INTEGER*2 FUNCTION CLICKQQ(ITEM)
   INTEGER*2 ITEM
END
```

This function takes one parameter: the menu item to be simulated. It returns a status of 0 if everything went well, or something besides 0 if there was a problem.

To help you understand your own code, Microsoft has supplied several **PARAMETER**s in FLIB.FD, any of which can be used as the parameter to CLICKQQ. These parameters include QWIN$STATUS, QWIN$TILE,

QWIN$CASCADE, and QWIN$ARRANGE; they simulate the Window menu options Status, Tile, Cascade, and Arrange Icons, respectively.

For even more control of the window placement in your application, the SETWSIZEQQ function allows your windows to be placed and sized exactly to your specifications. GETWSIZEQQ informs you of the current location and size of any child windows you have open. The interfaces to SETWSIZEQQ and GETSIZEQQ are described as follows.

```
STRUCTURE /QWINFO/
  INTEGER*2 TYPE            ! request type
  INTEGER*2 X              ! x coordinate for upper left
  INTEGER*2 Y              ! y coordinate for upper left
  INTEGER*2 H              ! window height
  INTEGER*2 W              ! window width
END STRUCTURE

INTERFACE TO INTEGER*2 FUNCTION SETWSIZEQQ(IUNIT,WINFO)
  INTEGER*2 IUNIT
  RECORD /QWINFO/ WINFO
END

INTERFACE TO INTEGER*2 FUNCTION GETWSIZEQQ(IUNIT,IREQ,WINFO)
  INTEGER*2 IUNIT
  INTEGER*2 IREQ
  RECORD /QWINFO/ WINFO
END
```

The IUNIT parameter of each function is the number of the unit in question (the **UNIT=** number from the **OPEN** statement). The QWINFO structure is used to pass information to and from QuickWin regarding the size and location of the window in question.

The X and Y fields in the QWINFO structure represent the position of the upper-left corner of the window within the application's main window. The H and W fields specify the height and width of the window. In the case of SETWSIZEQQ, these structure elements specify the size requested for the window. In GETWSIZEQQ, they contain the information about the window specified.

The TYPE parameter of SETWSIZEQQ is used to designate the action that should be taken. The symbolic constant QWIN$MIN requests that the specified child window be minimized. QWIN$MAX requests that the child window be maximized. QWIN$RESTORE returns a minimized or maximized child window to its original size. QWIN$SET is used to set the exact size and position of the window, as supplied in the X, Y, H, and W fields.

Finally, the IREQ parameter of GETWSIZEQQ indicates which window information is to be retrieved. There are four symbolic values that can be used here:

QWIN$CHILDCURR   Returns information about the current size of the specified child window.

QWIN$CHILDMAX   Returns information about the maximum possible size of the specified child window.

QWIN$FRAMECURR   Returns information about the current size and position of the application's window.

QWIN$FRAMEMAX   Returns information about the maximum possible size, and the current position, of the application's window.

 Note   The position and size information used with SETWSIZEQQ and GETWSIZEQQ is measured in terms of characters, since QuickWin is a text-based interface. Therefore, the height and width shown for each window is given as the number of character rows and columns available.

The following program demonstrates these calls. It opens three child windows, determines their current and maximum sizes, and displays this information within the windows. The UNIT=* window is then used to display the same information about the application window.

```
C    QW05.FOR
C    FORTRAN Program for Windows. This program starts up
C    under Windows and opens some child windows, giving each
C    window a title. The sizes of the windows and the main
C    application are determined and displayed.
C
C    Author:    L. John Ribar
C    Date:      11 Sept 1994
C    System:    MS FORTRAN 5.1
C    OS:        MS Windows

     INCLUDE 'FLIB.FI'                ! Interface descriptions

     Program QW05
```

```
        INTEGER*2   I                 ! Counting variable
        INTEGER*2   Status            ! Status from commands

        INCLUDE 'FLIB.FD'             ! Definitions
        RECORD /QWINFO/ MyWin

        OPEN( UNIT=10, FILE='USER', TITLE='QW 1', IOFOCUS =
       +    .TRUE.)
        OPEN( UNIT=11, FILE='USER', TITLE='QW 2', IOFOCUS =
       +    .TRUE.)
        OPEN( UNIT=12, FILE='USER', TITLE='QW 3', IOFOCUS =
       +    .TRUE.)

C       Tile the windows
        Status = CLICKQQ( QWIN$TILE )

C       Get info about other windows and display it
        DO I=10,12
           Status = GETWSIZEQQ( I, QWIN$CHILDCURR, MyWin )
           WRITE( I, 100 ) MyWin.X, MyWin.Y
           WRITE( I, 110 ) MyWin.H, MyWin.W
           Status = GETWSIZEQQ( I, QWIN$CHILDMAX, MyWin )
           WRITE( I, 120 ) MyWin.H, MyWin.W
        END DO

C       Now, display info about the Application window
        Status = GETWSIZEQQ( I, QWIN$FRAMECURR, MyWin )
        WRITE( *, 130 ) MyWin.X, MyWin.Y
        WRITE( *, 110 ) MyWin.H, MyWin.W
        Status = GETWSIZEQQ( I, QWIN$FRAMEMAX, MyWin )
        WRITE( *, 120 ) MyWin.H, MyWin.W

100     FORMAT(' I am at ',I3,', ',I3)
110     FORMAT(' My current size is ',I3,' by ',I3)
120     FORMAT(' My maximum size is ',I3,' by ',I3)
130     FORMAT(' Application is at ',I3,', ',I3)

        END                           ! End of program
```

The final output of this application is shown in Figure 3-6.

FIGURE
3-6

Displaying window sizes and positions

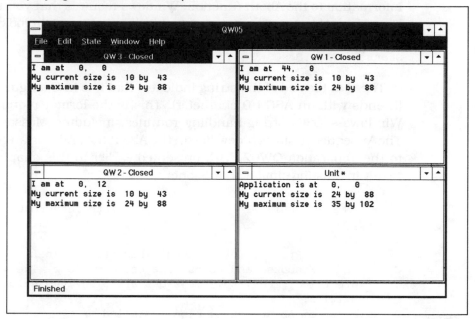

Message Boxes and About Boxes

With what you have learned, you could write a very useful, multi-window Windows application. However, QuickWin simplifies this programming for two frequently used window types. The first type, the About box, is shown to the user when the About option is selected from the Help menu. The second type, a message box, can be used to display information to the user and ask for specific responses.

The interfaces to these routines are shown here:

```
INTERFACE TO INTEGER*2 FUNCTION ABOUTBOXQQ(STR)
  CHARACTER*(*) STR
END

INTERFACE TO INTEGER*2 FUNCTION MESSAGEBOXQQ(MSG,CAPTION,MTYPE)
  CHARACTER*(*) MSG
  CHARACTER*(*) CAPTION
  INTEGER*2 MTYPE
END
```

To add an About Box of your own, all you have to do is send the textual information to the About function. Windows requires that you use the C string format to specify what your text is. Your entry might look like this:

```
Status = AboutBoxQQ('My Program 1.0\r John Ribar'C)
```

The C at the end of the string indicates that it is in C language format (it ends with an ASCII 0 character). This is the format required by all Windows-specific string-handling routines, including MessageBoxQQ. The \r sequence starts a new line in the About box. Adding an About box to the application QW02.FOR, presented earlier in this chapter, would result in a listing similar to this one:

```
        INCLUDE 'FLIB.FI'              ! Interface routines

C    QW02A.FOR
C    FORTRAN Program for Windows. This program starts up
C    under Windows, and opens some child windows. The windows
C    are tiled. Then, some messages are displayed before
C    exiting.
C    A custom About Box is also installed.
C
C    Author:    L. John Ribar
C    Date:      11 Sept 1994
C    System:    MS FORTRAN 5.1
C    OS:        MS Windows

        Program QW02A

        INCLUDE 'FLIB.FD'              ! Definitions
        INTEGER*2   Status             ! Status variable
        INTEGER*2   W                  ! Window number

        Status = AboutBoxQQ('   QW02A\rby John Ribar'C)

        OPEN( UNIT=10, FILE='USER')    ! Open the first child
        OPEN( UNIT=11, FILE='USER')    ! Open the second child
        OPEN( UNIT=12, FILE='USER')    ! Open the third child

C    Now, simulate the Window Tile menu command
        Status = CLICKQQ( QWIN$TILE )

C    Now, write to the windows. Notice that the default
C    window (with highlighted title) does not change as the
C    text is written into each window.
```

```
        W = 10
        DO WHILE (W .NE. 0)
            WRITE(*,*) ' Pick a window (10,11,12 or 0 to quit): '
            READ(*,'(I2)') W
            IF ( (W.LT.10).OR.(W.GT.12)) GOTO 200

            WRITE( W, * ) 'Writing to your window now!'
200     END DO

        END                                  ! End of program
```

The actual About box, selected from the Help menu's About option, appears as shown here:

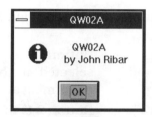

 Remember   All strings passed into Windows routines must be passed as C format strings, designated with the letter C at the end of the string itself, after the closing quote.

Message boxes are created to warn, question, or instruct users. A common box might say "Are you sure?", with the options Yes and No, as shown here:

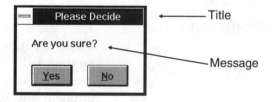

To create such a message box would require the following code:

```
    Status = MessageBoxQQ( 'Are you sure?'C,
  +  'Please Decide'C, MB$YESNO )
```

The first parameter is the question or information you wish for the user to see. The second parameter is the caption, or title of the message box. The third parameter is the value that determines the buttons and icons that will be shown. The following values are available:

Symbolic Value	Meaning
MB$IconAsterisk	The lowercase i icon (specifying information) is displayed.
MB$IconInformation	The lowercase i icon is displayed.
MB$IconExclamation	The Exclamation Point icon is displayed
MB$IconHand	The Stop Sign icon is displayed.
MB$IconStop	The Stop Sign icon is displayed.
MB$IconQuestion	The Question Mark icon is displayed.
MB$DefButton1	Button 1 is the default response, which is selected if the user presses ENTER without performing any other changes.
MB$DefButton2	Button 2 is the default response.
MB$DefButton3	Button 3 is the default response.
MB$Ok	An OK button is displayed.
MB$OkCancel	An OK and a Cancel button are displayed.
MB$RetryCancel	A Retry and a Cancel button are displayed.
MB$AbortRetryIgnore	Abort, Retry, and Ignore buttons are displayed.
MB$YesNo	Yes and No buttons are displayed.
MB$YesNoCancel	Yes, No, and Cancel buttons are displayed.
MB$TaskModal	The box is task modal, which means that all other processing within your program is suspended until the user responds to this message box, but that all other Windows applications will continue to execute.
MB$SystemModal	The box is system modal, which means that all other Windows applications will be suspended until the user responds to this message box.

Tip In FORTRAN, the case of identifiers does not matter, and the FD and FI files actually list all symbolic constants as all uppercase. The convention of using mixed upper- and lowercase letters, as shown here, makes the text somewhat more readable; this convention is not required.

These values can also be combined, using the IOR function or the .OR. operation, to provide other effects. For example,

```
MB$OK .OR. MB$ICONASTERISK
```

will use the OK button and the Information icon in the message box, as shown here:

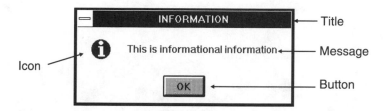

The return value of the message box is either 0 or the number of the button that was pushed. A value of 0 implies that there was not enough memory to create your message box. Any other value should be one of the following, based on the buttons you included in your message box:

Symbolic Value	Meaning
MB$IDAbort	The Abort button was pressed.
MB$IDCancel	The Cancel button was pressed.
MB$IDIgnore	The Ignore button was pressed.
MB$IDNo	The No button was pressed.
MB$IDOK	The OK button was pressed.
MB$IDRetry	The Retry button was pressed.
MB$IDYes	The Yes button was pressed.

Perhaps an entire application is now in order, showing you the use of the concepts presented thus far. The following program opens two child windows, displaying application information in one and a menu of options in the other. The UNIT=* window is used for asking the user to specify which menu option should be performed next. The program's output will make window 10 (labeled "Statistics") an icon; the result will look like Figure 3-7.

```
C     QW06.FOR

C     FORTRAN Program for Windows. This program starts up
C     under Windows and opens two child windows. One is used to
C     display information about the application. The other
C     displays a menu of selections for the user. A customized
C     About box is used, and message boxes are used to
C     communicate with the user.

C     Author:     L. John Ribar
C     Date:       11 Sept 1994
C     System:     MS FORTRAN 5.1
C     OS:         MS Windows

      INCLUDE 'FLIB.FI'              ! Interface routines

      Program QW06

      INTEGER*2   Status            ! Status Return variable
      INTEGER*2   Selection         ! User's selection
      INTEGER*2   MyUnit            ! Unit lookup
```

FIGURE 3-7   The result of minimizing a child window

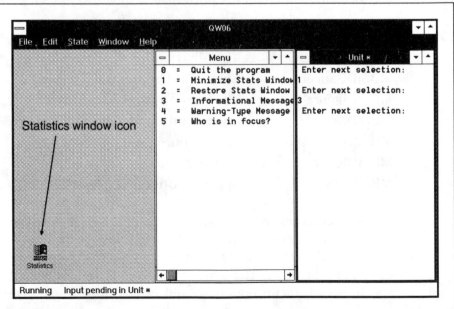

```fortran
         INCLUDE 'FLIB.FD'              ! Definitions
         RECORD /QWInfo/ MyWindow       ! Information about windows

C     Register the custom About box
         Status = AboutBoxQQ('QW06 Test Program\r by John Ribar'C)

C     Create two child windows
         OPEN( UNIT=10, FILE='USER', TITLE='Menu', IOFOCUS =
      +       .FALSE.)
         OPEN( UNIT=11, FILE='USER', TITLE='Statistics',
      +       IOFOCUS = .FALSE.)

C     Tile the windows, so they can be read.
         Status = ClickQQ( QWIN$Tile )

C     Now, write to the windows. First the menu, in window 10.
         WRITE( 10, * ) ' 0  =  Quit the program'
         WRITE( 10, * ) ' 1  =  Minimize Stats Window'
         WRITE( 10, * ) ' 2  =  Restore Stats Window'
         WRITE( 10, * ) ' 3  =  Informational Message'
         WRITE( 10, * ) ' 4  =  Warning-Type Message'
         WRITE( 10, * ) ' 5  =  Who is in focus?'

C     Display application information in window 11.
         Status = GetWSizeQQ( 0, QWIN$FRAMECURR, MyWindow )
         WRITE( 11, 101 ) MyWindow.Y, MyWindow.X
         WRITE( 11, 102 ) MyWindow.H, MyWindow.W
         Status = GetWSizeQQ( 0, QWIN$FRAMEMAX, MyWindow )
         WRITE( 11, 103 ) MyWindow.H, MyWindow.W

101   FORMAT(' Application is at row ',I3,', column ',I3)
102   FORMAT(' App Window is ',I3,' tall and ',I3,' wide')
103   FORMAT(' Maximum size is ',I3,' rows and ',I3,' columns')

C     Here, start the loop asking for user input.
         Selection = 1                  ! Default value

         DO WHILE (Selection .NE. 0)

C        Make sure the focus is in the input window. By FORTRAN
C        default, Unit 5 is the input file...
         Status = FocusQQ(5)

         WRITE(*,*) ' Enter next selection: '
         READ(*,'(I2)') Selection
```

```
            SELECT CASE (Selection)
C           Selection 0 = Quit
            CASE (0)
               Status = MessageBoxQQ(
     +                'Are you sure you want to stop?'C,
     +                'Just Checking...'C,
     +                MB$YesNo .OR. MB$IconQuestion .OR.
     +                MB$DefButton1)

C           If they don't want to quit, change the selection
            IF (Status .NE. MB$IDYes) Selection = 1

C           Selection 1 = Minimize Stats Window
            CASE (1)
              MyWindow.Type = QWIN$Min
              Status = SetWSizeQQ( 11, MyWindow )

C           Selection 2 = Restore Stats Window
            CASE (2)
              MyWindow.Type = QWIN$Restore
              Status = SetWSizeQQ( 11, MyWindow )

C           Selection 3 = Information message
            CASE (3)
               Status = MessageBoxQQ(
     +                'I am glad you are still here!'C,
     +                'Information'C,
     +                MB$IconInformation .OR. MB$OK )

C           Selection 4 = Warning message
            CASE (4)
               Status = MessageBoxQQ(
     +                'An error has occurred somewhere!'C,
     +                'WARNING!'C,
     +                MB$IconExclamation .OR.
     +                MB$AbortRetryIgnore )
            IF (Status .EQ. MB$IDIgnore) THEN
               WRITE(*,*) ' Ignoring an error could be
     +         dangerous.'
               WRITE(*,*) ' Good thing it was just a fake.'
            ELSE IF (Status .EQ. MB$IDAbort) THEN
               WRITE(*,*) ' I will not abort yet, because'
                  WRITE(*,*) ' this was not really an error!'
            ELSE IF (Status .EQ. MB$IDRetry) THEN
               WRITE(*,*) ' Retry all you want. There is not'
               WRITE(*,*) ' really anything wrong!'
            ELSE
```

```
                    WRITE(*,*) ' Unknown status ',Status,
        +              'arrived!'
                END IF

C        Selection 5 = Tell us who has the focus.
         CASE (5)
             Status = InqFocusQQ( MyUnit )
             WRITE(*,*) MyUnit, ' currently has the focus.'

C        Default case - the user didn't pick a valid choice.
         CASE Default
             Status = MessageBoxQQ(
        +              'Valid selections are 0 through 5!'C,
        +              'Selection Error'C,
        +              MB$IconStop .OR. MB$OK )
      END SELECT

   END DO

   END                                  ! End of program
```

Determining and Setting the Focus

One final topic concerning the text mode of QuickWin programs: There are times when you will want to know which window has the focus, and be able to focus on another window if required. These capabilities are provided by the following functions, included in the QuickWin library:

```
INTERFACE TO INTEGER*2 FUNCTION FOCUSQQ(IUNIT)
  INTEGER*2 IUNIT
END

INTERFACE TO INTEGER*2 FUNCTION INQFOCUSQQ(IUNIT)
  INTEGER*2 IUNIT
END
```

FOCUSQQ is used to set the focus to a specific window (again, using the unit number from the **OPEN** command). INQFOCUSQQ sets the IUNIT parameter to the unit number of the window currently in focus.

 Note   Why is focus important? If a window is not in focus, it cannot accept input from the user! There are three ways to change the focus other than through FOCUSQQ calls: by clicking the mouse in the window that should be in focus, by selecting the window from the Window menu, or by pressing CTRL-TAB to rotate through the windows that are currently available.

Both functions return 0 if everything has gone well. If there was a problem, usually caused by a closed window being in focus, a non zero value is returned.

Now that you can write text programs for Windows, your next step is learning how to add graphics. After all, Windows is a *Graphical* User Interface!

QuickWin Graphics

The QuickWin Graphics library was developed to help Microsoft FOR-TRAN programmers who had developed graphic display routines under PC-DOS or MS-DOS quickly port their programs to the Windows environment. Therefore, this section might at first seem most useful to those of you who have used Microsoft FORTRAN to develop your graphics programs. However, if you are writing new FORTRAN programs to take advantage of Windows, the graphics library will allow you to keep the same feel in your programs as in the text-mode programs you have written.

The building of graphics programs requires that the QWIN library be merged into your standard FORTRAN library. The documentation that comes with your compiler explains how this is done. Beyond this, compiling your graphics applications is as easy as compiling your text-mode QuickWin applications—just add the /MW option to your compilation command.

The first difference you will notice in code written for the QuickWin Graphics library is the use of the files FGRAPH.FI and FGRAPH.FD, rather than (or along with) the FLIB.FI and FLIB.FD files that were used in your text mode programs. FGRAPH.FI and FGRAPH.FD contain the interface and definition information necessary for use of the graphics functions. It is beyond the scope of this book to cover all the possible graphics possibilities available with Microsoft FORTRAN, but the major topics will be covered in the next few sections. First, though, you may want to review the features available from the standard QuickWin Graphics application menu.

The Basic QuickWin Graphics Window

As with the text-based QuickWin library, QuickWin Graphics provides a default application window and menu when a program is run. The FORTRAN code used to generate the window and menu is shown here:

```
C       QW01G.FOR
C       FORTRAN Program for Windows. Includes both Text and
C       Graphics child windows in the application.

        INCLUDE 'FGRAPH.FI'              ! Interface information
        INCLUDE 'FLIB.FI'

        Program QW01G

        INTEGER*2 Status                 ! Return status
        INCLUDE 'FGRAPH.FD'              ! Definitions
        INCLUDE 'FLIB.FD'

C       Write to the graphics window
        CALL OutText('Hello there!')

C       Now some output for the text window (Unit *)
        WRITE(*,*) ' This is in the text window.'

C       Tile the default text and graphics child windows so
C       they can be read easier.
        Status = ClickQQ( QWIN$Tile )

        END
```

The result of this code is shown in Figure 3-8.

A QuickWin graphics-based program automatically provides two windows—a text mode window and a graphics mode window. The text window can be manipulated with the functions you learned in the first half of this chapter. The graphics window can accept standard Microsoft graphics library commands.

FIGURE
3-8

A simple QuickWin graphics application

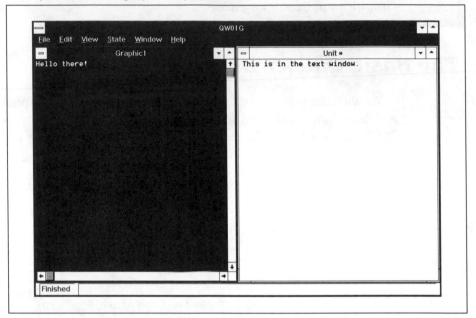

When the child windows are minimized, as shown in Figure 3-9, you will see that text and graphics windows are given different icons, thus helping you to find specific windows when you need them. Also, the menu is somewhat different from the text-only QuickWin menu; the differences are described in the next few sections.

The Graphics Edit Menu

For graphics windows, the Edit menu only has a Copy option available. This option copies the image in the window to the clipboard. From the clipboard, the image can be pasted into another Windows application, for printing or modification.

The Graphics View Menu

There are two special View menu commands available for graphics windows. The first, Size To Fit, causes all graphic drawing within a

FIGURE 3-9   QuickWin icons for text and graphics windows

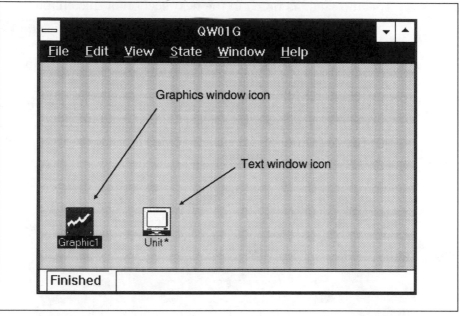

window to be done in such a way that the final image fits within the size of the window. Without this feature, the image could be much larger than the window, meaning that you'd need to use the scroll bars to look at different sections of the image. Once Size To Fit is selected, that menu option is marked with a check mark on the menu, and all drawings will be scaled to fit within the window. If you decide you want to use the original drawing scale, select Size To Fit again; the check mark will disappear, and graphic images will be resized to their original scale.

To see the entire image in full size, select the Full Screen option from the View menu. This option removes everything from the screen and draws your graphic image on the entire screen area. This feature is ideal for checking a drawing before copying it to the clipboard.

Standard Graphics Calls

If you have done graphics programming before in FORTRAN, especially if you have used the Microsoft Graphics library, you should feel right at home with the QuickWin Graphics library. There are only a few Windows-specific calls, as noted in the next section of this chapter.

One nice aspect of the QuickWin Graphics library is that you can see both a text window and a graphics image at the same time on the screen. For instance, in Figure 3-10 you see a text input window next to a graphics display window.

Most of the code in the next example is standard graphics and FORTRAN text processing. The only Windows-specific call is included to tile the two windows for easier viewing of their respective data. The code for this program is shown here:

```
C       QW02G.FOR
C       FORTRAN Program for Windows. Includes both Text and
C       Graphics child windows in the application.
C       Performs drawings in the
C       graphics window based on input from the text window.

        INCLUDE 'FGRAPH.FI'              ! Interface information
        INCLUDE 'FLIB.FI'
```

FIGURE 3-10   A QuickWin graphics program using text and graphics windows

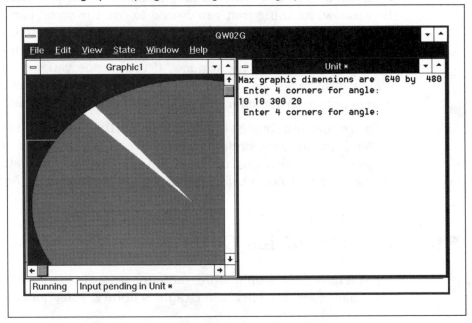

```
          Program QW02G

          INTEGER*2 Status              ! Return status
          INTEGER*2 angX1, angY1        ! Display angle start
          INTEGER*2 angX2, angY2        ! Display angle end
          INTEGER*2 MaxX, MaxY          ! Size of display area
          INTEGER*2 MainUnit            ! Unit * ID

          INCLUDE 'FGRAPH.FD'           ! Definitions
          INCLUDE 'FLIB.FD'

          RECORD /VideoConfig/ VideoInfo

    C     Determine the Unit=* window handle
          Status = InqFocusQQ( MainUnit )

    C     Select the video mode with best resolution
          Status = SetVideoMode($VRes16Color)
    C     Retrieve the video setup information
          CALL GetVideoConfig( VideoInfo )
          MaxX = VideoInfo.NumXPixels
          MaxY = VideoInfo.NumYPixels

    C     Register fonts and pick a standard type style
          Status = RegisterFonts("dummy string")
          Status = SetFont("t'modern'")

    C     Select the color for outgtext()
          Status = SetColor($LightCyan)
    C     Now clear the window
          CALL ClearScreen($GWindow)
    C     And write out some text.
          CALL OutGText('Hello there!')

    C     Tile the default text and graphics child windows so
    C     they can be read easier.
          Status = ClickQQ( QWIN$Tile )

          WRITE(*,101) MaxX, MaxY
    101   FORMAT(' Max graphic dimensions are ',I4,' by ',I4)

    C     Give focus to text window for input
          Status = FocusQQ( MainUnit )

          WRITE(*,*) ' Enter 4 corners for angle: '
          READ (*,'(4I4)') angX1, angY1, angX2, angY2
          DO WHILE ((angX1 + angX2) .GT. 0.0)
```

```
C       Put up a clean background
        CALL ClearScreen($GWindow)        ! Clear window first
        Status = SetColor($LightCyan)
        Status = Rectangle_W( $GBorder, 0, MaxY/4, MaxX,
     +          MaxY-(MaxY/4) )

C       Next, draw the pie part.
        Status = SetColor($Yellow)
        Status = Pie_W( $GFillInterior, 10, 10, MaxX-10,
     +          MaxY-10, angX1, angY1, angX2, angY2 )
        Status = SetColor($Red)
        Status = Pie_W( $GFillInterior, 10, 10, MaxX-10,
     +          MaxY-10, angX2, angY2, angX1, angY1 )

C       Get the next one to draw.
        WRITE(*,*) ' Enter 4 corners for angle: '
        READ (*,'(4I4)') angX1, angY1, angX2, angY2
      END DO

      END
```

Unfortunately, looking at Figure 3-10, you cannot completely see the image in window Graphic1. To view the entire picture, make the Graphic1 window active (by clicking in the window with your mouse or selecting it from the Window menu), then select Size To Fit from the View menu. Now each time the drawing changes, it will be drawn to fit within the window. The output will look like Figure 3-11, and you will better recognize the image being drawn.

Windows-Specific Graphics Calls

There are only a few Windows-specific calls in the QuickWin graphics library. These involve opening and closing graphics windows (WGOpenQQ and WGCloseQQ), setting and checking the window focus (WGSetActiveQQ and WGGetActiveQQ), and retrieving keystrokes from within graphic windows (InCharQQ). The interface statements for these functions are as follows.

```
INTERFACE TO INTEGER*2 FUNCTION WQOPENQQ(NAME)
  CHARACTER*(*) NAME
END
```

```
INTERFACE TO INTEGER*2 FUNCTION WGCLOSEQQ(HANDLE)
  INTEGER*2 HANDLE
END

INTERFACE TO INTEGER*2 FUNCTION WGGETACTIVEQQ()
END

INTERFACE TO INTEGER*2 FUNCTION WGSETACTIVEQQ(HANDLE)
  INTEGER*2 HANDLE
END

INTERFACE TO INTEGER*2 FUNCTION INCHARQQ()
END
```

Graphics windows are opened somewhat differently than text windows. Text windows use the **OPEN** command, with USER as the filename; you, as the programmer, specify the unit number. Graphics windows are opened with a call to WGOpenQQ. The only parameter is the title to be placed on the window. (Remember to use a C format string.) This function returns a *handle* to the window that is created. (A handle is a number,

Sizing the drawing with Size To Fit

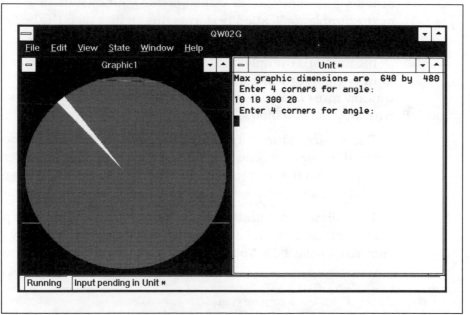

generated by Windows, that is used to track the window.) A return value of 0 signifies that the window could not be created.

After you complete the use of a graphics window, a call to WGCloseQQ, passing in the handle of the window to be closed, is all that is required to remove the window.

Once a graphics window has been opened, you need to set the focus on that window before you can work with it. This is done with a call to WGSetActiveQQ, passing the handle of the window that should become active. If successful, this function returns a value of 1. A 0 value signifies that errors have occurred.

 Note   Passing a handle value of –1 to WGSetActiveQQ causes all the currently open graphics windows to be made inactive, thus shutting down the graphics processing for your application.

If you need to know which graphics window is currently active, make a call to WGGetActiveQQ. The return value from this function is the handle of the currently active window. A return value of –1 signifies that no graphics windows are active.

Since the QuickWin system always creates a graphics window named Graphic1, you may wish to use the WGGetActiveQQ and WGCloseQQ functions to remove it, and then create your own named windows. The next example application performs this change near the beginning of the program's execution.

InCharQQ is the only means by which character input can be retrieved from a graphics window. In order for InCharQQ to work, the graphics window must have the focus; a character can only be retrieved from the currently active window.

The return value of InCharQQ is the ASCII value of the keystroke pressed by the user. The character is not echoed to the screen, however, so if you want the user to see what was typed, you'll have to use the text display routines available in the graphics library.

The following application uses many of these Windows-specific calls, along with some standard graphics library calls, to display the images shown in Figure 3-12. Notice that each window appears in Size To Fit mode.

```
C      QW03G.FOR
C      FORTRAN Program for Windows. Creates several new graphics
```

FIGURE
3-12

Graphic images in multiple windows

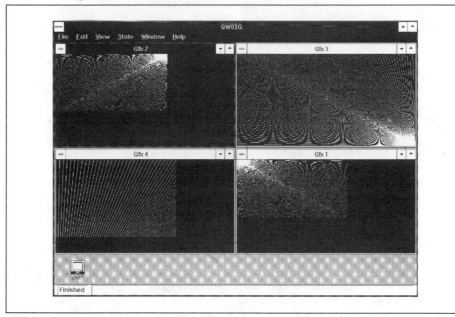

```
C       child windows in the application. Performs drawing in the
C       graphics windows.

        INCLUDE 'FGRAPH.FI'             ! Interface information
        INCLUDE 'FLIB.FI'

        Program QW03G

        INTEGER*2 Status                ! Return status
        INTEGER*2 I, J                  ! Loop variables
        INTEGER*2 MaxX, MaxY            ! Size of display area
        INTEGER*2 MainUnit              ! Base text handle
        INTEGER*2 MainHandle            ! Base graphics handle
        INTEGER*2 w1, w2, w3, w4        ! Child handles

        INCLUDE 'FGRAPH.FD'             ! Definitions
        INCLUDE 'FLIB.FD'

        RECORD /XYCoord/    LastCoord
        RECORD /QWInfo/     MyTextWin
```

```
C       Determine the Unit=* window handle and minimize it
        Status = InqFocusQQ( MainUnit )
        MyTextWin.Type = QWIN$Min
        Status = SetWSizeQQ( MainUnit, MyTextWin )

C       Determine base graphics window handle, and close it
        MainHandle = WGGetActiveQQ()
        Status = WGCloseQQ( MainHandle )

C       Set maximum values, based on VGA resolution
        MaxX = 639
        MaxY = 479

C       Open four display windows
        w1 = WGOpenQQ( 'Gfx 1'C )
        w2 = WGOpenQQ( 'Gfx 2'C )
        w3 = WGOpenQQ( 'Gfx 3'C )
        w4 = WGOpenQQ( 'Gfx 4'C )

C       Select the color for drawing
        Status = SetColor($LightCyan)

C       Tile the default text and graphics child windows so
C       they can be read easier.
        Status = ClickQQ( QWIN$Tile )

        DO I=1,4                          ! For each window
          SELECT CASE (I)

            CASE (1)
C               Activate the window and set the video mode
                Status = WGSetActiveQQ( w1 )
                Status = SetVideoMode($MaxColorMode)
C               Select the color for drawing
                Status = SetColor($LightCyan)
                DO J=0,MaxY,10
                    CALL MoveTo( 0, 0, LastCoord )
                    Status = LineTo( MaxX, J )
                END DO
                DO J=MaxX,0, -10
                    CALL MoveTo( 0, 0, LastCoord )
                    Status = LineTo( J, MaxY )
                END DO

            CASE (2)
C               Activate the window and set the video mode
                Status = WGSetActiveQQ( w2 )
```

```
                        Status = SetVideoMode($MaxResMode)
C                       Select the color for drawing
                        Status = SetColor($Yellow)
                        DO J=0,MaxY,10
                            CALL MoveTo( MaxX, 0, LastCoord )
                            Status = LineTo( 0, J )
                        END DO
                        DO J=0,MaxX,10
                            CALL MoveTo( MaxX, 0, LastCoord )
                            Status = LineTo( J, MaxY )
                        END DO

                CASE (3)
C                       Activate the window and set the video mode
                        Status = WGSetActiveQQ( w3 )
                        Status = SetVideoMode($VRes16Color)
C                       Select the color for drawing
                        Status = SetColor($Brown)
                        DO J=MaxY,0,-10
                            CALL MoveTo( MaxX, MaxY, LastCoord )
                            Status = LineTo( 0, J )
                        END DO
                        DO J=0,MaxX,10
                            CALL MoveTo( MaxX, MaxY, LastCoord )
                            Status = LineTo( J, 0 )
                        END DO

                CASE (4)
C                       Activate the window and set the video mode
                        Status = WGSetActiveQQ( w4 )
                        Status = SetVideoMode($MRes256Color)
C                       Select the color for drawing
                        Status = SetColor($LightRed)
                        DO J=0,MaxX,10
                            CALL MoveTo( 0, MaxY, LastCoord )
                            Status = LineTo( J, 0 )
                        END DO
                        DO J=0,MaxY,10
                            CALL MoveTo( 0, MaxY, LastCoord )
                            Status = LineTo( MaxX, J )
                        END DO

            END SELECT
        END DO

        END
```

Coming Attractions

One of the major advances of Windows is that pieces of code that are used by many applications can be shared, with only one copy of the code being loaded in memory, even if the applications are all running at the same time. This feature is provided by means of the Dynamic Link Libraries (DLLs). DLLs are covered in Chapter 5, but first, Chapter 4 discusses the WATCOM FORTRAN compiler.

CHAPTER

Using the WATCOM FORTRAN Compiler

*I*n Chapters 2 and 3, the Microsoft FORTRAN compiler was discussed. There is another option for Windows programmers: the WATCOM FORTRAN compilers for 16- and 32-bit programming. WATCOM has combined the ability to use your existing FORTRAN code, with standard FORTRAN input and output functions, with the ability to make use of the full Windows API (Application Programming Interface) In this chapter, you'll see how these features can be used. The chapter begins with a brief introduction to the WATCOM compiler and concludes with a discussion of the use of the Windows API. Realize, however, that this book is not intended to address every aspect of the Windows API. For more thorough coverage of the API, consult some of the books listed in the section, "Additional Sources of Information," located just before Chapter 1 of this book.

Using Your Existing FORTRAN Code

WATCOM has refined their existing compiler to allow FORTRAN applications to be compiled and run under Windows with little or no alteration. In addition, with minor modifications, you can extend your programs to make use of more Windows-specific capabilities.

Compiling Existing Code

The major place in FORTRAN code where changes need to occur for Windows is in the handling of input and output. Like Microsoft, WATCOM provides a means of running existing FORTRAN-based text programs under Windows.

Let's say you've written a simple calculation program to add numbers together until a zero is entered, and then to print the average. The code might look like this:

```
C       WAverage.FOR
C
C       Program to calculate the average of a series of
C       numbers.
C
C       Author:        L. John Ribar
```

```
C       Date:           29 Sept 1994
C       System:         WATCOM FORTRAN 9.1
C       OS:             DOS/Windows
C

        PROGRAM WAverage

        INTEGER*2   Count       ! Number of items read
        INTEGER*4   Total       ! Total amount collected
        INTEGER*2   aNumber     ! Latest Number Entered

        WRITE(*,*) ' Enter numbers to be averaged, 0 to quit:'
        Count = 0
        Total = 0

10      CONTINUE
        WRITE(*,*) 'Number: '
        READ(*,20) aNumber
20      FORMAT(I3)
        IF (aNumber .NE. 0) THEN
          Total = Total + aNumber
          Count = Count + 1
          GOTO 10
        END IF

        WRITE(*,100) Count, Total
100     FORMAT(' Total of ',I3,' items was ',I5)

        WRITE(*,110) Total/Count
110     FORMAT(' Average of the numbers was ',I4)

        END
```

Compiling this program for Windows, using the WATCOM system, involves the following steps. First, compile the program using one of the following commands. (The **wfc** command is for protected mode compilation, available only to 80386 or larger processors.)

```
wfc WAVERAGE /fpc /win
wfcp WAVERAGE /fpc /win
```

The **/fpc** command tells the compiler to use the floating-point libraries, and **/win** instructs the compiler to generate object files compatible with Windows.

Next, use the WATCOM linker to generate the Windows application with the following command:

```
wlink sys windows mem font op st=8k, heap=4k f WAverage
```

This creates an application called WAVERAGE.EXE. When it is run under Windows, the result looks like Figure 4-1.

Since the linker command tends to get quite long, WATCOM allows you to place all your linker commands, or directives, in a *linker directive file*. The contents of the file for this example might look like this:

```
SYSTEM Windows Memory Font
OPTIONS Stack=8k, Heap=4k
FILE WAverage
```

Save these statements in a file called WAVERAGE.LNK. Now, to call the linker, you'll use this command:

```
wlink @WAverage.LNK
```

A program built in this way makes use of the WATCOM Default Window System. This is a generic window package that provides a

FIGURE 4-1

A simple WATCOM FORTRAN Windows program

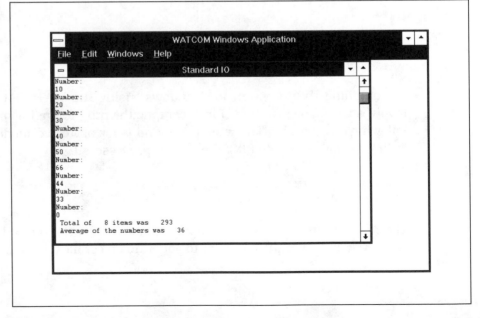

standard menu system and windowing interface for your programs. (See Figure 4-1.) There are four menu items provided: File, Edit, Windows, and Help.

The WATCOM File Menu

The File menu offers three options: Save As, Set Lines Between Auto-Clears, and Exit.

Save As is used to save the contents of the currently selected window in a text file for later review. If your program only uses the Standard I/O window, this is the window that will be captured. If you are using additional windows, as described in the next section, you will need to select the window you want to save before choosing this menu option.

Tip   The simplest way to select a window is by clicking the left button of your mouse while pointing to the window. An alternate method is by selecting the name of the window from the Windows menu.

Set Lines Between Auto-Clears sets the number of lines that will be saved for each of your console windows, including Standard I/O. The number that you enter will be valid for each window you have open. That is, if you select a buffer of 1000 lines, then 1000 lines will be saved for each of the windows you have open.

The Exit option is used to end the application and close its window.

The WATCOM Edit Menu

The Edit menu has two options: Copy and Clear. The Copy command is used to copy the contents of the current window into the clipboard, which can then be pasted into other Windows applications (Microsoft Word for Windows and Microsoft Excel, for instance) that make use of this buffer.

The Clear option is used to clear all the information from the currently selected window. This command can only be used after the application has stopped execution.

The WATCOM Windows Menu

The Windows menu gives as options a list of the windows that are currently in use by the application. The first item in this list, unless it has been closed, will always be Standard IO, followed by Console 1, Console 2, and so on. Selecting one of these menu choices makes the appropriate window active.

The WATCOM Help Menu

The Help menu only allows selection of the About option. This option displays the WATCOM Default Windowing System copyright and version information in a dialog box. Clicking the OK button with your mouse returns you to your application.

Refining User Interface with Console Windows

You can make your text-mode FORTRAN programs more functional (and more user-friendly) by opening separate windows to contain separate files. You create these windows, called *console windows*, by using the filename CON when you open the files. The next two statements will open additional windows for your program, accessed as files 10 and 11:

```
OPEN(File='CON', UNIT=10)
OPEN(File='CON', UNIT=11)
```

Now, any input (**READ**) or output (**WRITE**) directed toward files 10 or 11 will happen within these new windows. Using this arrangement, you can keep separate parts of your program available to the user at any given time.

The following example displays a menu in one window, but generates the output in the second and third, as shown in Figure 4-2.

```
C       W3Wins.FOR
C       FORTRAN Windows Program to show the use of multiple
C       input and output windows.

C       Author:      L. John Ribar
C       Date:        29 Sept 1994
```

```fortran
C       System:         WATCOM FORTRAN 9.1
C       OS:             MS Windows

        PROGRAM w3Wins

        INTEGER*2    InChoice          ! User menu selection
        INTEGER*2    InUse             ! Unit for Output
        INTEGER*2    MsgCount          ! Count of Msgs Displayed

C       Remember, first window open is for UNITs 5/6
        OPEN( UNIT=10, FILE='CON' )    ! Open 2nd Window
        OPEN( UNIT=11, FILE='CON' )    ! Open 3rd Window
        OPEN( UNIT=12, FILE='CON' )    ! Open 4th Window

C       Display the menu in default window
        WRITE(*,*) ' MENU'
        WRITE(*,*) ' 1. Display Messages'
        WRITE(*,*) ' 2. Output to Window 11'
        WRITE(*,*) ' 3. Output to Window 12'
        WRITE(*,*) ' 4. Exit'

C       Default output to window 11
        InUse = 11

100     CONTINUE
        WRITE(10,*) ' Enter selection: '
        READ(10,101) InChoice
101     FORMAT(I2)

        SELECT (InChoice)
          CASE (1)
            GOTO 110
          CASE (2)
            GOTO 120
          CASE (3)
            GOTO 130
          CASE (4)
            GOTO 140
        END SELECT
        WRITE(10,*) ' Valid selections are 1 through 4, please.'
        GOTO 100

110     CONTINUE ! Output to the currently selected window
        WRITE( InUse, 111 ) MsgCount
        MsgCount = MsgCount + 1
111     FORMAT(' Message ',I3,' was here!')
        GOTO 100
```

```
120     CONTINUE ! Change output window to Unit 11
        InUse = 11
        GOTO 100

130     CONTINUE ! Change output window to Unit 12
        InUse = 12
        GOTO 100

140     CONTINUE ! Quit
        WRITE( *, * ) ' Thanks... '

        END
```

Note Although you may number your units 10, 11, and 12, the WATCOM Default Window System assigns them titles, beginning with Console 1 (for the first window you open). The default window (for units 5/6) is named Standard IO. (See Figure 4-2.)

 A multi-window application using WATCOM FORTRAN

FIGURE 4-2

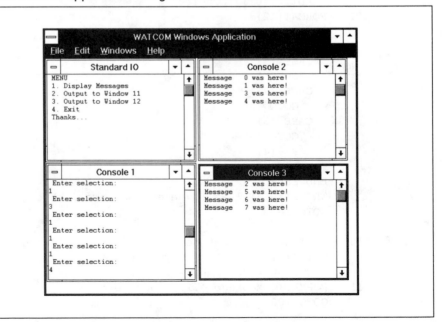

Using the Windows API

Both WATCOM and Microsoft allow you to bring existing FORTRAN code into the Windows environment with a minimum of effort, using the WATCOM Default Windowing System and Microsoft QuickWin Libraries.

However, if you really want to get into the depths of Windows programming, you'll want to learn more about the Windows API. This is a set of functions, available to all Windows applications, that handle all the user-interface details. WATCOM FORTRAN allows the use of the API, as discussed here.

 Note   This is by no means a complete coverage of the Windows API. If you'd like to know more about Windows API programming, look into the books listed in the section entitled "Additional Sources of Information" at the beginning of this book.

A New Way of Programming

One of the major reasons this book is not about Windows API programming is the shift in programming structure that would be required. While this is all interesting information, it wouldn't be very useful for helping you downsize your existing code. Once you have FORTRAN code running under Windows, you may want to go back and learn more about the specific API calls.

Windows is structured around a message-based system of programming known as the event-driven programming paradigm. Native Windows programs (those that make use of the API functions) do not look like the FORTRAN programs you grew up with. Why not?

Unlike programs created in more structured programming languages and environments, Windows applications do not always follow a strict sequence of steps. This is because the user has several ways to interact with applications (such as the keyboard, mouse, menus, and buttons), and because several applications can be running at the same time. All the user interaction is handled by Windows, not by your application!

What happens, therefore, is that your program usually sits around idle, waiting for Windows to tell it when the user has done something. If the user resizes a window, your program might need to redraw the image that was displayed there. If a menu selection is made, your program will be informed, so that the correct procedures can be performed.

This may sound somewhat inside-out. After some practice and experience, though, programming in the Windows environment becomes like second nature. However if your goal is downsizing, and not rewriting, all your FORTRAN programs, you should probably try the other opportunities in this book before heading too deeply into Windows API programming.

Calling API Functions

To give you a better feel for what a native Windows program looks like, here is an example WATCOM FORTRAN program, written to use the Windows API. Note that the FI files (provided by WATCOM) that are included in this application detail the interfaces to the Windows API functions.

The program listing, shown here, incorporates one of WATCOM's example programs, with comments added for this book by the author.

```
! Ellipse.FOR
! Windows Program to Display Ellipses
! Author:        WATCOM
! System:        WATCOM FORTRAN 9.1

! Include the Windows API interface details
*$include winapi.fi

! Each Windows program must have a function called FWinMain.
! This function is called directly by Windows to start up
! the application. The parameters are also fixed, as specified
! by Microsoft. In a C language program, you would see the
! function WinMain().

c$noreference
        integer*2 function FWINMAIN( hInstance,
     &                               hPrevInstance,
     &                               lpszCmdLine,
     &                               nCmdShow )
c$reference

        integer*2 hInstance
```

```
            integer*2 hPrevInstance
            integer*2 nCmdShow
            integer*4 lpszCmdLine

            include 'win386.fi'
            include 'wincreat.fi'
            include 'wincurs.fi'
            include 'windefn.fi'
            include 'windisp.fi'
            include 'winmsg.fi'
            include 'winmsgs.fi'
            include 'windtool.fi'
            include 'winutil.fi'

            external WndProc

            integer*2          hWnd
            record /MSG/        msg
            record /WNDCLASS/   wndclass
            character*14        class

!           The first step in a pure Windows program is to define
!           the window you will be using and then register the
!           new window "class," create the window, open it (placing
!           the border on the screen), and update it (fill it with
!           the information or drawing that is expected).

! Define the Window Class
  wndclass.style = CS_HREDRAW .or. CS_VREDRAW
!   The WndProc is a procedure called by Windows whenever an
!   event occurs that is actually associated with this
!   application. You'll see that the procedure (WndProc)
!   that handles the events is defined later in this file.
!   At this point, give the location (address) of the procedure
!   to Windows, through the window class setup.
  wndclass.lpfnWndProc = loc( WndProc )
  wndclass.cbClsExtra = 0
  wndclass.cbWndExtra = 0
  wndclass.hInstance = hInstance
  wndclass.hIcon = NULL_HANDLE
  wndclass.hCursor = LoadCursor( NULL_HANDLE, IDC_ARROW )
  wndclass.hbrBackground = GetStockObject( WHITE_BRUSH )
  wndclass.lpszMenuName = NULL
  write( class, '(''Ellipses'',i5.5,a)' ) hInstance, char(0)
  wndclass.lpszClassName = Loc( class )

! Register the class with Windows
```

```
      if( RegisterClass( wndclass ) .eq. 0 )then
          FWINMAIN = 0
          return
      end if

! Create a window of the class just registered
          hWnd = CreateWindow( class,
     &                         class,
     &                         WS_OVERLAPPEDWINDOW,
     &                         CW_USEDEFAULT,
     &                         0,
     &                         CW_USEDEFAULT,
     &                         0,
     &                         NULL_HANDLE,
     &                         NULL_HANDLE,
     &                         hInstance,
     &                         NULL )

! Now show the window, and update its contents
          call ShowWindow( hWnd, nCmdShow )
          call UpdateWindow( hWnd )

! Each Windows program has a loop, similar to this one, in
! which the application waits for messages (known as EVENTS)
! from Windows and then acts upon them. In this case, if
! no message is waiting to be acted upon, draw another
! ellipse on the screen (within our window, of course).

          loop
              if( PeekMessage( msg, NULL_HANDLE, 0, 0,
     &                         PM_REMOVE ) .ne. 0 )then
                  if( msg.message .eq. WM_QUIT ) exit
                  call TranslateMessage( msg )
                  call DispatchMessage( msg )
              else
                  call DrawEllipse( hWnd )
              endif
          endloop

! Now exit the application
          FWINMAIN = msg.wParam

          end


! This is the subroutine called from within the main
! application message-processing loop. Because of where
```

```fortran
! it is called, and how often, make sure these routines
! don't get too long. Windows acts multitasking, but
! an application can keep control as long as it wants.

      subroutine DrawEllipse( hWnd )

      integer*2 hWnd

      include 'win386.fi'
      include 'windefn.fi'
      include 'winellps.fi'
      include 'windtool.fi'
      include 'winpaint.fi'
      include 'winutil.fi'

      external            irand
      integer*2           irand

      integer*2           hBrush
      integer*2           hDC
      integer*2           xLeft, xRight, yTop, yBottom
      integer*2           nRed, nGreen, nBlue
      integer*2           xClient, yClient

      common /client/ xClient, yClient

      xLeft   = mod( irand(), xClient )
      xRight  = mod( irand(), xClient )
      yTop    = mod( irand(), yClient )
      yBottom = mod( irand(), yClient )
      nRed    = irand() .and. 255
      nGreen  = irand() .and. 255
      nBlue   = irand() .and. 255

      hDC = GetDC( hWnd )
      hBrush = CreateSolidBrush( RGB( nRed, nGreen, nBlue ) )
      call SelectObject( hDC, hBrush )

      call Ellipse( hDC, min( xLeft, xRight ),
     &                   min( yTop, yBottom ),
     &                   max( xLeft, xRight ),
     &                   max( yTop, yBottom ) )

      call ReleaseDC( hWnd, hDC )
      call DeleteObject( hBrush )

      end
```

```
!    Here is the callback function called by Windows whenever
!    an event occurs for this window. Here, handle all the
!    events that you are worried about.

*$pragma aux (callback) WndProc parm( value, value, value,
     &     value )

       integer*4 function WndProc( HWnd, iMessage, wParam,
     &     lParam )

       integer*2 hWnd
       integer*2 iMessage
       integer*2 wParam
       integer*4 lParam

       include 'win386.fi'
       include 'windefn.fi'
       include 'winmsg.fi'
       include 'winmsgs.fi'
       include 'winutil.fi'
       include 'wincreat.fi'

       integer*2      xClient, yClient

       common /client/ xClient, yClient

!      Process, based on the message passed in
       select( iMessage )
       case( WM_SIZE )          ! This is a RESIZE WINDOW Event
           xClient = LOWORD( lParam )
           yClient = HIWORD( lParam )
       case( WM_DESTROY )
!          This is when the program stops
           call PostQuitMessage( 0 )
       case default             ! Otherwise, use Window's
                                ! defaults
           WndProc = DefWindowProc( hWnd, iMessage, wParam,
     +         lParam )
           return
       end select

       WndProc = 0

       end

!    This is a local routine used to generate random numbers, to
```

```
!   display a more pleasing set of ellipses.

        integer*2 function irand()

        integer         seed
        real            urand

        data seed/75347/

        irand = int( urand( seed ) * 32767 )

        end
```

The output of the program is shown in Figure 4-3.

What About C?

Do you need to use C to write Windows applications? No; as you've just seen, WATCOM FORTRAN allows full access to the Windows API functions.

FIGURE
4-3

A graphical API example program

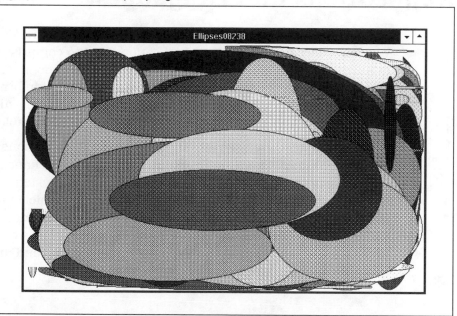

Should you learn C? This question deserves an affirmative answer. You might never use C as a programming language, but the documentation now available on Windows programming, both in manuals and in magazines and trade journals, generally includes C and C++ language examples. Most shareware and public domain source code available for Windows programming is provided in C or C++. If you learn enough C to read the examples, adding Windows functions to your FORTRAN applications will be much simpler.

In addition, incorporating C language examples into your programs through DLLs or mixed-language programming will be much easier if you know something about the C language.

There are several tools that can help you learn C, including a book written especially for FORTRAN programmers trying to learn C, and a program that converts FORTRAN code to C. Details on these products, and on others that may help, are given in the "Additional Sources of Information" section located just before Chapter 1.

Using FORTRAN with Other Applications and Languages

This book is a guide to using your existing FORTRAN code with Windows, to form stand-alone applications and to comprise libraries of existing code that can be shared by many applications. Because of this emphasis on FORTRAN, you won't find a great deal of information here about writing Windows programs that make use of the API calls; as mentioned earlier, there are other excellent sources available for that.

Thus far, you have been introduced to writing applications using your existing FORTRAN code, with minimal source code changes, to make better use of the Microsoft and WATCOM windowing systems. In the next chapter, you'll learn how to create and use Dynamic Link Libraries (DLLs). DLLs provide other applications and programming languages with access to the functions you write in FORTRAN. DLLs can allow this access even from within BASIC and C programs, and from within commercial applications such as spreadsheet packages.

CHAPTER

Dynamic Link
Libraries

One of the most important advances available within the Windows environment is Dynamic Link Libraries (DLLs). DLLs are a great method for saving disk and memory space and for controlling distribution of libraries. In this chapter, you'll learn the hows and whys of implementing FORTRAN-based DLLs for use in your Windows applications.

Why Use DLLs Anyway?

You have probably used a *static linker* to build most of your non-Windows programs. This means that as a program was compiled, the entire set of software required to make that program run (object files and libraries) was combined into the executable file by the linker. A static linker creates one big file that can be passed to your friends and associates.

With a *dynamic linker* and *Dynamic Link Libraries*, some of the software, usually one or more of your libraries, is not linked to the program at link time; in fact, the software is not combined until it actually runs! Windows handles this dynamic loading of software at run time automatically, without your knowledge as a user. As a programmer, however, you probably should know more about these special Dynamic Link Libraries.

There are many reasons to use DLLs, but not all compilers allow the use of all their capabilities. In this section, you will learn the reasons behind using DLLs, and constraints of using DLLs with specific compilers. Later in this chapter, you will learn how to build your own Dynamic Link Libraries using FORTRAN.

Tapping the Capabilities of DLLs

When you create a set of subroutines and functions that are useful to many applications, you will often group them into libraries, which can be linked into any new programs you write. Windows Dynamic Link Libraries provide several distinct advantages over using standard library files:

☐ DLLs can be used from any language or application running in Windows that has a DLL interface. In this way, you can write applications that use libraries written in FORTRAN, Pascal, and C++, without worrying too much about which language was used for a specific piece of code. This flexibility extends to DLLs created with compilers from different software vendors—a feat nearly unheard of before now. In fact, some programmers are putting useful DLLs into the public domain or releasing them as shareware. The prices of useful library software, compatible with multiple compilers and languages, are starting to come down!

☐ DLLs are only loaded one time by Windows. This means that, even if you have ten different programs that use your newest algorithm, they need only one copy of the code in memory, even when they all run at the same time! Sharing code between applications greatly conserves system memory.

☐ Although a single copy of code in a DLL can be shared between applications, the data is usually not shared. When you build DLLs, you can specify that the data areas should be shared, or that a new data area should be created for each user. Separate data areas mean that each user can share the code, but perform the functions on their own data. On the other hand, if you want data to be shared between applications, this can also be established through a DLL.

☐ You can designate that DLLs *not* be shared. This restriction is often made in applications written for a single user, to prevent the user from running the application on a network, with other people, all sharing the same DLL.

☐ You can save a great deal of disk space. If you create a super text-manipulation library and want to use it in all your programs, you will need only one copy of the code on disk (in the DLL). Each of your applications will therefore be smaller, because only a link to the DLL code, not a copy of the code itself, will exist within each application's EXE file.

☐ Linking time is reduced, since only the link to the DLL is required. The entire code of your library does not have to be read from the disk and then copied into your executable file, as would normally be done with a static linker.

☐   Updating your libraries is much simpler and quicker. If you create, or purchase, a library of common routines that are used by many of your applications, you can update all the applications by just replacing the single DLL file. There is no need to recompile or relink all your applications, unless the functions within the DLL have changed the way in which they are called. Many software vendors are pleased with this approach; as they update their libraries, they only need to send you a new DLL file—no installation is required other than copying the new DLL file to your DLL directory.

Limitations of Microsoft FORTRAN DLLs

Microsoft FORTRAN allows the creation of Dynamic Link Libraries for use in Windows. In this way, many of the FORTRAN algorithms you have developed over the years can be migrated into the Windows environment. However, the Microsoft compiler has a few restrictions on the DLLs that can be created.

☐   Only computational algorithms and file access can be performed with Microsoft FORTRAN DLLs. No screen manipulation can be performed.

☐   The QuickWin text and graphics libraries cannot be used within a DLL.

☐   Multiple instances of FORTRAN DLLs cannot exist. This restriction stems from the requirement that MS FORTRAN files be compiled with the large memory model. Windows DLLs cannot have multiple data segments, which happens when they are built using the large memory model.

☐   The FORTRAN run-time library must be linked with the DLLs that are created. This is not a major problem, but it does cause DLLs to be somewhat larger than necessary. In addition, if you create multiple DLLs, each one of them must include a copy of the run-time library; the Microsoft FORTRAN run-time library cannot be created as a DLL.

Creating and Using Dynamic Link Libraries

Writing the code for a DLL is no different than writing code for a standard application or a static library. What is different is the way in which your applications are linked together. As mentioned earlier, a static library is linked to your application during the link step of compilation. A *dynamic* library (DLL) is linked dynamically at run time; during the link step, only the information about the DLL is attached to your application.

To create a DLL, you first need to compile the code to enable specific Windows capabilities. You then use the linker to create the actual DLL file. In order for the linker to know how you want the DLL built, a DEF file is required.

DEFinition Files

The Microsoft FORTRAN compiler comes equipped with a default definition (DEF) file. This file is called FL.DEF, and is located in the FORTRAN BINB directory. If you are compiling a DOS application, the FL command knows that no DEF file is required. If you are compiling a Windows application or a DLL, and you haven't specified a DEF file, FL.DEF will be used.

DEF files are simply ASCII files, built with your normal editor (like PWB). Because of their importance, you should understand what they contain. Shown here is the FL.DEF file included by Microsoft. (The comments included are also from Microsoft.)

```
;
; FL.DEF - Default .def file for FORTRAN Windows applications
;
; Copyright (C) Microsoft Corp 1991. All rights reserved.
;

NAME            WINDOWAPI

;
```

```
; The NAME statement tells the linker that a Windows
; application is being built. The linker supplies the actual
; name of the application from the base name of the executable
; file.
;

APPLOADER          '__MSLANGLOAD'


;
; The APPLOADER statement pulls in an alternate application
; loader from the FORTRAN library which the application uses
; instead of the normal Windows loader. This new loader fixes
; a bug in the normal Windows loader that prevents huge data
; items from being loaded properly. This statement should be
; used in all applications built with FORTRAN 5.1 for Windows
; 3.0.
;

EXETYPE            WINDOWS 3.0


;
; The EXETYPE statement tells the linker to build a Windows
; 3.0 executable file. This statement should be used in all
; applications built with FORTRAN 5.1 for Windows 3.0.
;

STUB               'WINSTUB.EXE'


;
; The STUB statement pulls in an executable file which is run
; when the application is run independently of Windows 3.0.
; WINSTUB.EXE displays the message 'This program requires
; Microsoft Windows' when executed.
;

PROTMODE


;
; The PROTMODE statement tells the linker to mark the
; application for execution in Windows standard or enhanced
; mode.
;

CODE               PRELOAD MOVEABLE DISCARDABLE
DATA               PRELOAD MOVEABLE


;
```

```
; The CODE and DATA statements set the attributes of the
; applications CODE and DATA segments. See Chapter 22 in the
; Environment and Tools manual for a complete description of
; the options for these statements.
;

HEAPSIZE        1024
STACKSIZE       8096

;
; The HEAPSIZE and STACKSIZE statements set the applications
; near heap and stack sizes. The values specified are
; recommended for QuickWin applications. See Chapter 22 in the
; Environment and Tools manual for a complete description of
; these statements.
;


;
; Uncomment these lines for DLL module definition file model.
;
;EXPORTS
; WEP


;
; The above section should be uncommented if this .DEF file is
; to be used as a model for a FORTRAN 5.1 dynamic-link library
; (DLL) .DEF file. The WEP routine is included in the FORTRAN
; 5.1 startup code, but the symbol must be explicitly exported.
; If a DLL already has a user-defined WEP routine, the routine
; should be renamed _WEP. The startup code will call _WEP,
; if present, during DLL termination. For additional
; information concerning the WEP function, see the Windows 3.0
; SDK documentation.
;
```

In order to make the best use of DEF files, you should first understand the commands that are available.

NAME and LIBRARY

The **NAME** and **LIBRARY** statements are used to give the final linked output a name and an application type. **NAME** is used with applications (EXE files), and **LIBRARY** is used when DLL files are created. Therefore, these commands cannot both be used within the same DEF file.

NAME and **LIBRARY** are followed by one or two parameters, in any order. One parameter is the name of the application or library being created. If no name is specified, the name is taken from the link statement.

For **NAME**, a second parameter defines the type of application being created. **WINDOWAPI** specifies that the output from this link will be an application that uses the Windows API and runs as a standard Windows application. The other options are **WINDOWCOMPAT**, which creates a program that can run within a text window in the Windows environment, and **NONWINDOWCOMPAT**, which creates a program that only runs in a full-screen, non-windowed mode.

The **LIBRARY** command uses the **PRIVATELIB** command, as shown here:

```
LIBRARY    MyLib PRIVATELIB
```

PRIVATELIB designates that the DLL can only be used by a single application.

If neither **NAME** nor **LIBRARY** appears in a DEF file, the default action will be to create a **WINDOWAPI** application, named from the linker command line.

DESCRIPTION

A **DESCRIPTION** statement can be used to better document what is being created. A **DESCRIPTION** statement is different from a comment line, which begins with a semicolon (;), in that **DESCRIPTION** information is actually embedded into the executable or library file. A typical use of this command is for adding copyright or revision information, as shown here:

```
DESCRIPTION 'Julian Date DLL, (c) 1994 PSGL. Rev 1.01'
```

The description can be up to 255 characters, and must be surrounded by a set of single or double quotes. If no **DESCRIPTION** command is given, the name of the application, as specified in the linker command line, will be embedded instead.

APPLOADER

Windows normally handles the loading of applications and DLLs. In some cases, you might need to provide your own application loader. This is actually required with Microsoft FORTRAN applications and those making use of QuickWin libraries; for these applications and DLLs, use the following **APPLOADER** command:

```
APPLOADER      '__MSLANGLOAD'
```

This application loader is provided with the Microsoft FORTRAN run-time libraries.

EXETYPE

EXETYPE commands are used to specify the operating system for which the application or library is being built. The default **EXETYPE** is **WINDOWS**, creating an application that only runs under the Windows operating system. When using **WINDOWS** as the **EXETYPE**, you can also specify the minimum version of Windows required to allow the application to run. For instance, to allow any version of Windows past 2.0 to run an application, you would use this command:

```
EXETYPE    WINDOWS 2.0
```

The default version number, if none is specified, is 3.0, meaning that at least version 3.0 of Windows must be in use for the application to execute.

The alternatives for **WINDOWS** as an **EXETYPE** are **DOS** and **UNKNOWN**. **DOS** creates a DOS program, and **UNKNOWN** creates a program with no specific bits set. This type of program cannot be run directly from DOS or Windows.

With **WINDOWS** executable applications, two additional commands, **PROTMODE** and **REALMODE**, are possible; they are described next.

PROTMODE and REALMODE   These commands are optionally specified with Windows programs. **PROTMODE** is the default; it tells the linker that the application can only run under protected modes of Windows. These are the extended versions of Windows, which require additional memory, but which allow better response and greater capabilities. Many programs now require protected mode.

REALMODE informs the linker that the application can run under any mode of Windows, including real mode. This is a restricted mode of Windows, which is more compatible with the older versions, but which does not handle memory or other resources as efficiently. **REALMODE** implies that protected mode can also be used.

Note   Real-mode programming is the type of programming done in DOS, where you have access to the real memory of the system. In protected mode, the operating system (or environment, as is the case with Windows) protects each application from bothering the other applications. Real-mode programming is not common for Windows, and its support is dwindling with each release.

If a **PROTMODE** or **REALMODE** command is required, it is usually placed alone on the line after the **EXETYPE** command, as shown here:

```
EXETYPE Windows 3.0
PROTMODE
```

PROTMODE and **REALMODE** cannot be used together; only one of the commands can be used in any one DEF file.

STUB

The **STUB** command is used to specify the name of a DOS program to be linked into the application or DLL. This program will be run if the application is started under DOS. The DOS program is specified after the **STUB** keyword, surrounded by single or double quotes.

While the stub program is normally just a message informing the user to use Windows, it can actually be any DOS program. In fact, you could write both DOS and Windows versions of your application, and through WINSTUB, create a program that runs under either operating environment automatically.

Optionally, the command

```
STUB NONE
```

tells the linker not to include any stub program. This reduces the size of your final executable or library file. Unfortunately, your system will hang if the program is mistakenly run under DOS.

CODE and DATA

The **CODE** and **DATA** commands are used to specify how Windows is allowed to manipulate the code and data portions of the application. Following the **DATA** and **CODE** keywords are a series of attribute values. The **CODE** attributes are called *discard, executeonly, load, moveable,* and *shared.* The **DATA** attributes are called *instance, load, moveable, readonly,* and *shared.* Their functions are described in Table 5-1.

TABLE 5-1

The Possible Values of CODE and DATA Attributes

Attribute	Value	Purpose
Discard (CODE)	DISCARDABLE	Allows Windows to discard the memory for the specified segment of code if it is required by another application. When the memory is needed by Windows later, it will be reloaded.
	NONDISCARDABLE	Causes Windows to keep the specified code segment loaded once it is in memory until it is no longer required by any applications. (Default attribute.)
Executeonly (CODE)	EXECUTEONLY	Indicates that the specified segment of code can only be executed, not read. This prohibits debuggers from following the progress of the application.
	EXECUTEREAD	Allows applications, such as debuggers, to execute and also read the code in the segment. (Default.)

TABLE 5-1	The Possible Values of CODE and DATA Attributes (*continued*)		
Attribute	**Value**		**Purpose**
Instance (DATA)	NONE		Indicates that no memory should be allocated for the specified data segment. This attribute is used when there are no memory requirements for the DLL itself.
	SINGLE		Indicates that the data segment should be allocated and shared by all instances of the DLL. (Default for DLLs.)
	MULTIPLE		Creates a data area for each application that uses the DLL. (Default for applications.)
Load (both)	PRELOAD		Causes Windows to load the DLL code and data as soon as the application begins.
	LOADONCALL		Prevents Windows from loading the DLL until it is actually called for from the application. (Default.)
Moveable (both)	MOVEABLE		Allows Windows to move a specified code or data segment within memory, if required. This attribute is only used for real-mode applications and DLLs.
	FIXED		Instructs Windows not to move the code or data within memory. (Default.)
Readonly (DATA)	READONLY		Indicates that the data can only be read, not changed by any applications.
	READWRITE		Allows applications to both read and write to the data segment.

TABLE 5-1 The Possible Values of CODE and DATA Attributes (*continued*)

Attribute	Value	Purpose
Shared (both)	SHARED	This attribute is used for real-mode Windows; it allows all applications to share a common code segment. (Default for DLLs.)
	NONSHARED	Forces Windows to load a copy of the code for each application that requires it. (Default for applications.)

The default attributes used by Microsoft FORTRAN applications are listed here:

```
CODE        PRELOAD MOVEABLE DISCARDABLE
DATA        PRELOAD MOVEABLE
```

HEAPSIZE and STACKSIZE

The **HEAPSIZE** and **STACKSIZE** commands are used to manage the amount of memory available to applications for specific purposes. **HEAPSIZE** specifies the size of the local heap designated for an application or DLL. If **HEAPSIZE** is not specified, no heap will be created. The recommended minimum size for Windows programs is 1024 bytes.

STACKSIZE determines the size of an application's stack. It is not used with DLLs. For most Windows applications, a minimum stack size of 5120 is recommended; Microsoft FORTRAN recommends at least 8096.

IMPORTS and EXPORTS

The **IMPORTS** and **EXPORTS** statements are used to specify the interfaces between DLLs and applications.

In the DEF file of a DLL, **EXPORTS** is used to list the routines that can be accessed from outside the DLL. These routines are listed following the **EXPORTS** statement, separated by spaces or placed on separate lines. Any routines in the library that are not identified as **EXPORTS** will only be available from within the DLL.

In an application's DEF file, **IMPORTS** lists the names of those routines that are required from outside sources (DLLs).

Examples showing the use of **IMPORTS** and **EXPORTS** are presented in the next section of this chapter.

Using DEF Files to Create Applications

To create and use DLLs, you first needed to learn about definition files. These are the method by which DLLs are actually created and then used.

Suppose that you found a set of Julian Date routines that you wanted to use in several of your Windows applications. The code might be written like this:

```
C-------------------------------------------------------C
!      Julian.FOR
!
!      Julian Date Calculation Routines Library
!
!      Author:      L. John Ribar
!      System:      Microsoft FORTRAN 5.1
!      Date:        15 October 1994
!      OS:          DOS or Windows
!
!      These routines are based on a personal interpretation
!      of how Julian dates should work. While the "real"
!      Julian dates are not calculated exactly the same way,
!      the numbers generated here can be used for the same
!      purposes in most cases.
!
C-------------------------------------------------------C


!      Julian() returns the Julian date for a given date.
!
       REAL*4 FUNCTION Julian( Year, Month, Day )
```

```
        INTEGER*2 Year, Month, Day

        REAL*4    TotalDate
        INTEGER*2 DayOfYear        ! Function return type

!       First, determine days through the beginning of the
!       year. Years have about 365.2425 days each.
        TotalDate = Year * 365.2425

!       Now, add the days that have occurred in this year.
        TotalDate = TotalDate + DayOfYear( Year, Month, Day )

!       Finally, return the answer
        Julian = AINT(TotalDate)

        END                        ! FUNCTION Julian

C-----------------------------------------------------------C


!
!       CalendarDate() takes a given Julian date and returns
!       the actual calendar date, meaning month, day, and
!       year.
!
        SUBROUTINE CalendarDate( JulDate, Year, Month, Day )
        REAL*4    JulDate
        INTEGER*2 Year, Month, Day

        REAL*4    LeftOver
        INTEGER*2 LOver

!       Since years have about 365.2425 days each, determine
!       the years that are in this Julian number.
        Year = AINT( JulDate / 365.2425 )

!       To determine the month and day, subtract the year,
!       and call the MonthAndDay() subroutine.
        LeftOver = JulDate - AINT(365.2425 * Year)
        LOver = AINT(LeftOver)
        CALL MonthAndDay( LOver, Year, Month, Day )

!       That's All!
        END                        ! SUBROUTINE Calendar Date

C-----------------------------------------------------------C


!
```

```
!       WeekDayNo() returns the weekday of the Julian date
!       passed as a parameter. The first day of the week is
!       Sunday, which returns a 1. Thus, Saturday returns 7.
!

        INTEGER*2 FUNCTION WeekDayNo( JulDate )
        REAL*4    JulDate

        REAL*4    Temp

!       First, get the offset of the date, 0 = Friday
        Temp = MOD( JulDate, 7 )

!       Now adjust for actual weekdays
        Temp = Temp - 1
        IF (Temp.LE.0) Temp = Temp + 7
        WeekDayNo = Temp

        END                            ! FUNCTION WeekDayNo

C--------------------------------------------------------------C

!
!       The DayOfYear() function returns the day of the year
!       that corresponds to the month and day passed into
!       the routine.
!

        INTEGER*2 FUNCTION DayOfYear( Year, Month, Day )
        INTEGER*2 Year, Month, Day

        LOGICAL*2 IsLeap           ! Function return value
        LOGICAL*2 LeapYear
        INTEGER*2 I, J             ! Count/Sum variables
        INTEGER*2 Days(12)         ! Monthly offsets

!       This array holds the number of days of the previous
!       month, used to determine the days that have passed
!       in the year in question.
        DATA Days / 0, 31, 28, 31, 30, 31,
     +              30, 31, 31, 30, 31, 30 /

!       Adjust for leap years
        LeapYear = IsLeap(Year)
        IF (LeapYear) THEN
           Days(3) = 29
        END IF

!       Now add up the days that have passed
```

```
        J = Day                   ! Start with Day of Month
        DO I=1,Month              ! Add for each month
          J - J + Days(I)
        END DO

        DayOfYear = J

        END                       ! FUNCTION DayOfYear()

C----------------------------------------------------------C


      !
      !     The IsLeap() function returns TRUE if the year in
      !     question is a leap year, and FALSE otherwise.
      !
        LOGICAL*2 FUNCTION IsLeap( Year )
        INTEGER*2 Year

        INTEGER*2 By4, By100, By400

        By4   = MOD(Year,4)
        By100 = MOD(Year,100)
        By400 = MOD(Year,400)

        IF ( ((By4.EQ.0).AND.(By100.NE.0)) .OR.
      +      (By400.EQ.0)) THEN
           IsLeap = .TRUE.
        ELSE
           IsLeap = .FALSE.
        END IF

        END                       ! FUNCTION ByLeap()

C----------------------------------------------------------C
      !
      !     MonthAndDay() determines the month and day of a
      !     given annual day number.
      !
        SUBROUTINE MonthAndDay( DayNum, Year, Month, Day )
        INTEGER*2 DayNum, Year, Month, Day

        INTEGER*2 Days(12)        ! Monthly offsets
        INTEGER*2 DN              ! Calculatron
        LOGICAL*2 IsLeap          ! Function return type
        LOGICAL*2 LeapYear
```

```
!      This array holds the number of days of each month,
!      used to determine the days that will pass in each.
       DATA Days / 31, 28, 31, 30, 31, 30,
      +             31, 31, 30, 31, 30, 31 /

!      Adjust for leap years
       LeapYear = IsLeap(Year)
       IF (LeapYear) THEN
          Days(2) = 29
       END IF

!      Now count down the days for each month
       DN = DayNum
       Month = 1

       DO WHILE (DN .GT. Days(Month)) ! Still not right month
          DN = DN - Days(Month)
          Month = Month + 1
       END DO
       Day = DN

       END                          ! SUBROUTINE MonthAndDay

C------------------------------------------------------------C
```

Writing the code is only the first step. Now, to create the object code, compile the code using the following command:

```
FL /Gw /Aw /c Julian.FOR
```

The /Gw switch tells the compiler to generate Windows-specific epilogue and prologue code. The /Aw switch tells the compiler that the DLL cannot assume the data segment and stack are in the same place, because of the way Windows manages memory. Both of these switches are required.

Now that the code has been compiled, you need to create a definition (DEF) file. Here is what you might create in this case:

```
; Julian.DEF
; This is a linker definition file for the Julian date DLL
; By John Ribar  -  21 Sept 1994  -  Microsoft FORTRAN 5.1

LIBRARY     JULIAN
DESCRIPTION 'DLL for Julian Dates'
APPLOADER   '__MSLANGLOAD'
EXETYPE     WINDOWS 3.0
```

```
CODE         PRELOAD MOVEABLE DISCARDABLE
DATA         PRELOAD MOVEABLE SINGLE
HEAPSIZE     1024
EXPORTS
    Julian
    CalendarDate
    WeekDayNo
    WEP
```

You can now see how the EXPORTS command is used in the DEF file. It lists all the routines that will be available from outside the DLL. The WEP routine is supplied by the Microsoft FORTRAN compiler in the standard libraries, and is required for all Microsoft FORTRAN DLLs.

Finally, you need to use the linker to create the DLL file itself. When you run the linker in command mode, your screen might look like this:

```
C:\> LINK

Microsoft (R) Segmented-Executable Linker  Version 5.15
Copyright (C) Microsoft Corp 1984-1991. All rights reserved.

Object Modules [.OBJ]: JULIAN
Run File [JULIAN.EXE]: JULIAN.DLL
List File [NUL.MAP]:
Libraries [.LIB]: /NOD LDLLFEW.LIB
Definitions File [NUL.DEF]: JULIAN.DEF

C:\>
```

There it is! You've created your very own DLL. Now, how do you use it from within an application? Well, another DEF file is in order, this time for your application. Here is a simple test application for the Julian DLL:

```
C
C   TestJul2.FOR
C   FORTRAN program to test Julian date difference routines.
C
C   Author:     John Ribar
C   Date:       22 Sept 1994
C   System:     Microsoft FORTRAN 5.1
C   OS:         DOS/Windows
C
```

```
          PROGRAM TestJul2

          INTEGER*2    myD1, myM1, myY1    ! User selected date 1
          INTEGER*2    myD2, myM2, myY2    ! User selected date 2
          REAL*4       days                ! Days difference
          REAL*4       Julian              ! External function
          REAL*4       myJulian1           ! Converted Date 1
          REAL*4       myJulian2           ! Converted Date 2

          WRITE(*,*) ' Enter the first date ( MM DD YYYY ):'
          READ(*,101) myM1, myD1, myY1
          WRITE(*,*) ' Enter the second date ( MM DD YYYY ):'
          READ(*,101) myM2, myD2, myY2
  101     FORMAT(I2, 1X, I2, 1X, I4)

  C       Adjust for leaving the 1900 off the year
          IF (myY1 .LT. 100) myY1 = myY1 + 1900
          IF (myY2 .LT. 100) myY2 = myY2 + 1900

  C       Calculate the Julian dates
          myJulian1 = Julian( myY1, myM1, myD1 )
          myJulian2 = Julian( myY2, myM2, myD2 )

          IF (myJulian1 .GT. myJulian2) THEN
            days = myJulian1 - myJulian2
          ELSE
            days = myJulian2 - myJulian1
          END IF

          WRITE(*,102) days
  102     FORMAT(' There are ',F6.0,' days between those dates.')

          END
```

Caution There are two libraries being used in the creation of DLL-based applications. LLIBFEW.LIB is the standard Microsoft FORTRAN library for Windows programs. LDLLFEW.LIB is used when linking DLLs; it contains the run-time code required by the DLLs. Be sure you use the correct library in your link commands, or your applications will not work properly.

To compile this application, use the /MW and /c switches with the FL compiler. (The /MW switch was used in Chapters 2 and 3 for creating Windows applications.)

You need to use the /c switch here, because it tells the compiler not to link the application yet; that will be done next. Create a definition file (TESTJUL2.DEF) that looks like this:

```
; TestJul2.DEF
; This is a linker definition file for the Julian date test
; program
; By John Ribar  -  21 Sept 1994  -  Microsoft FORTRAN 5.1

NAME        TESTJUL2
DESCRIPTION 'Julian Dates Tester'
APPLOADER   '__MSLANGLOAD'
EXETYPE     WINDOWS 3.0
STUB        'WINSTUB.EXE'

CODE        PRELOAD MOVEABLE DISCARDABLE
DATA        PRELOAD MOVEABLE SINGLE
HEAPSIZE    1024
STACKSIZE   5120
IMPORTS     JULIAN.Julian
IMPORTS     JULIAN.CalendarDate
```

Note This definition file shows the use of the **IMPORTS** statement. The routines you need are listed with the DLL name and the routine name, connected by a period. While this system is fairly simple when used in smaller applications (like this one), it can become rather cumbersome in applications requiring many DLL routines. In the next section, you'll learn how to avoid entering lengthy series of **IMPORTS** statements by using the IMPLIB program.

You're almost finished! Just link the application, and you'll be done. Here is the screen you'll end up with:

```
C:\> LINK

Microsoft (R) Segmented-Executable Linker  Version 5.15
```

```
Object Modules [.OBJ]: TESTJUL2
Run File [TESTJUL2.EXE]:
List File [NUL.MAP]:
Libraries [.LIB]: /NOD LLIBFEW.LIB
Definitions File [NUL.DEF]: TESTJUL2.DEF

C:\>
```

Now you have a Windows program, written with FORTRAN, that uses a DLL you created. To run the application, first copy the DLL file JULIAN.DLL to your Windows directory. (This is where Windows will look for DLL files.) Then type **WIN TESTJUL2** to start up Windows and your program.

Using IMPLIB to Simplify the Distribution of DLLs

As noted above, adding a large number of **IMPORTS** statements to every DEF file you create can become quite cumbersome. If you don't mind adding another step to the building process, there is a way to reduce the number of **IMPORTS** you'll need in your application definition files.

Microsoft supplies a program called IMPLIB.EXE. IMPLIB reads your DLL, or your DLL's DEF file, and creates a LIB file that contains all the interface information. In this way, you can just link your application with the LIB file, like any other FORTRAN library, and not worry about listing all the **IMPORTS** in your DEF file.

If you plan to distribute your DLLs, IMPLIB-generated LIB files can be included with your DLLs, and no definition files will be required. This will also simplify the use of your DLL by others.

Creating Applications with IMPLIB Libraries

To actually generate the application TESTJUL2 using IMPLIB requires the following steps.

Once the DLL file has been created, run IMPLIB. You will need to specify the name of the LIB file to be created, and the name of the DEF or DLL file or files that should be included. (You can actually put the definitions for several of your favorite DLLs in one LIB file!)

Now, remove the IMPORTS statements from your application's DEF file. In the program above, this would involve the following lines of TESTJUL2.DEF:

```
IMPORTS       JULIAN.Julian
IMPORTS       JULIAN.CalendarDate
```

Finally, link your application. Make sure to include the new library file along with LLIBFEW.LIB, as shown here:

```
LINK TESTJUL2,TESTJUL2.EXE,NUL,/NOD JULIAN.LIB LLIBFEW.LIB,TESTJUL2.DEF
```

This entire command must be entered on a single DOS command line. It lists all the parameters on the command line of LINK. You can also run the linker without any command line parameters by answering the questions, as was done in the first attempt.

Creating DLLs with WATCOM FORTRAN

The WATCOM FORTRAN compiler can also be used to create DLLs from your existing code. In this section, you'll see how the equivalent of a Microsoft definition file is implemented within the WATCOM programming environment.

WATCOM allows you to list all linker commands, or *directives*, in a directive file, which is read by the linker. This is an ASCII text file, like the Microsoft DEF files, and contains similar commands to the DEF files discussed above. A standard list of WATCOM linker directives might include the following:

```
#   Standard Windows Linker Directives
    libpath %WATCOM%\lib286
    libpath %WATCOM%\lib286\win
    library windows
```

```
option stack=8k, heapsize=1k
format windows
```

This example comes from the WLINK.LNK example file provided by WATCOM with their compiler. These and other pertinent directives are discussed next.

Note that within WATCOM directive files, a comment is denoted by a pound symbol (#) in the first column.

PATH and FILE

PATH and **FILE** are used to specify the locations and names of application-specific code that should be linked together. Library files are specified using the **LIBPATH**, **LIBFILE**, and **LIBRARY** directives.

PATH specifies the path that should be searched to find the files listed with the **FILE** directive. The **FILE** directive lists all the OBJ files that should be included in the link process.

LIBPATH, LIBFILE, and LIBRARY

LIBPATH specifies the name of the directory, or directories, in which the WATCOM linker should look for the files specified in **LIBFILE** and **LIBRARY** directives; **LIBPATH** should therefore precede **LIBFILE** and **LIBRARY** in the directive file.

LIBFILE is used to list the OBJ file or files that should be linked into the application. **LIBRARY** similarly lists LIB files that need to be included. The set of directives shown here

```
LIBPATH c:\watcom\lib
LIBNAME app1, app1a
LIBRARY appbase
```

would instruct the linker to look for the following files:

```
c:\watcom\lib\app1.obj
c:\watcom\lib\app1a.obj
c:\watcom\lib\appbase.lib
```

Multiple **LIBPATH**, **LIBFILE**, and **LIBRARY** directives may be given in a directive file.

OPTION

OPTION commands all follow the keyword **OPTION** on the directive line, as illustrated in the examples below.

Note   The OPTION directive has a great number of possible uses. The most common, and most immediately useful, are shown here. For more information, see your WATCOM Linker manual.

The **DESCRIPTION** option is similar to the **DESCRIPTION** option used in Microsoft's DEF files—it inserts the provided text into the application. This option is often used for embedding copyright or version information, like this:

```
OPTION DESCRIPTION 'Julian Date Library V1.0 (c) 1994 PSGL'
```

The **HEAPSIZE** and **STACKSIZE** options provide the sizes of the heap and stack space that should be provided for the application. A standard configuration might look like this:

```
OPTION STACK=8k, HEAPSIZE=1k
```

The **MODNAME** option is used to specify the name of the application, or module, being created. **MODNAME** is often used to name DLLs when they are being built. If a **MODNAME** directive is not given, the name of the application comes from the first object file being linked.

The **STUB** option is used to select the DOS program to be included in the application and run when the program is started outside of Windows.

```
OPTION STUB=MyStub.EXE
```

Caution   The stub filename should not be the same as the application file that is being created.

FORMAT

Like the Microsoft **EXETYPE** command, **FORMAT** tells the WATCOM linker what sort of application file is being created. The formats you will most likely need to remember are shown in this table:

Directive	Purpose
FORMAT DOS	Creates a DOS application.
FORMAT WIN	Creates a Windows application.
FORMAT WIN FONT	Creates a Windows application that has the ability to use proportional fonts.
FORMAT WIN DLL	Creates a Windows DLL file.
FORMAT WIN DLL INITGLOBAL	Creates a Windows DLL file. Initialization of the DLL takes place once, when the DLL is first loaded.
FORMAT WIN DLL INITINSTANCE	Creates a Windows DLL file. Initialization of the DLL is called each time a new application requests the use of the DLL.

There are additional directives which are used in the creation of applications for OS/2, Novell, PharLap, and QNX environments.

NAME

The **NAME** directive is used to give the application a name. This is important to use when you create DLLs, because WATCOM's linker will assume an extension of EXE if not specified with the **NAME** directive. To assign a name, use a statement like this:

```
NAME Julian.DLL
```

IMPORT and EXPORT

IMPORT and **EXPORT** directives are used in WATCOM as they are in Microsoft DEF files, to list the names of functions that are being imported from a DLL or exported by a DLL. One or more **IMPORT** or **EXPORT** directives may be used in any one directive file.

DEBUG

The **DEBUG** directive is used to control the types of debugging information that will be generated for specific object modules.

Note   The DEBUG directive only affects the FILE and LIBRARY directives which follow it! Therefore, placing DEBUG at the end of your directive file will have no effect.

You must remember to also compile the files that you want to debug with the correct /d options. Otherwise, the linker will not be able to find the information it needs in the OBJ files.

Using FORTRAN with Other Application Sets

So far, you have been learning about using FORTRAN to write Windows programs. While this is a worthwhile endeavor in itself, there are also many other ways to use your FORTRAN code in Windows.

Now that you can create DLLs from your FORTRAN libraries, you can use these DLLs with several commercially available Windows applications. This ability enhances the value of your investment in coding FORTRAN algorithms, not only for programs that you write, but for use within programs that others have written. In the next chapter, you'll begin to learn how this is done.

CHAPTER

FORTRAN
Programming with C

*T*his chapter has two goals. The first is to give you a basic introduction to how C programs look, thus preparing you to learn the specifics of interfacing C with your FORTRAN programs. The second goal is to show you how FORTRAN and C routines can be mingled to create Windows applications.

An Introduction to C

C can be both a very simple and a very difficult language to learn. The simplest C program is very small:

```
main() {}
```

If you were to run this program, you would see that it doesn't do anything; however, it is a valid C program. Before going on, you must understand the parts of this simple program.

Each function in C has a name (like **main**), two parentheses, and two curly braces. If there are parameters to be sent into the function, they are listed within the parentheses. The actual program code for the function is placed between the curly braces.

C programs consist of one or more functions, each of which performs a sequence of events. Every C program begins with a function called **main()**. This is where program execution begins, and therefore the **main()** function is required in every C program.

Note A *function* is a group or sequence of C statements that are executed together, similar to a FUNCTION in FORTRAN. However, C differs from FORTRAN in that the term *function* in C refers both to functions that return a value (like FORTRAN FUNCTIONs) and to those that do not return a value (like FORTRAN SUBROUTINEs). The keywords FUNCTION and SUBROUTINE are not actually used in C. In most C literature, when a function is discussed, it is usually shown with the parentheses. This denotes that it is a function name, as opposed to a variable name. So the main function in a C program is shown as **main()**, not **main**.

Unlike many other languages, such as FORTRAN, in which the main routine usually has the same name as the program file, C requires all programs to start with the function **main()**. However, no requirements are placed on the filename used to hold the **main()** function; it can be any valid DOS filename, usually ending with the C extension.

The **main()** function can take an optional set of parameters. These parameters are used for reading the DOS command line and environment. A program with parameters for the **main()** function looks like this:

```
main ( int argc, char *argv[] )
{
}
```

The first parameter is defined with **int argc**. This declares **argc** to be an **int**eger variable. **char *argv[]** is a bit more complex; this is a declaration of **argv** as an array of character strings.

Note that the curly braces, { and }, have no code between them. Normally, the actual program code would go inside those braces.

C Basics

Here is another C program; while it is still simple, it actually does something.

```
/* A small C program to print a message to the screen. */
/* Written by L. John Ribar. */

#include <stdio.h>

main()
{
    printf("Hello again! \n");
}
```

The following step-by-step listing of the program will help you see how the C language performs each of the required functions. A C program usually begins with a comment, like this:

```
/* A small program to print a message to the screen */
/* Written by L. John Ribar. */
```

These two comments tell what the program is and who wrote it.

While they are shown as two comments in the preceding example, the text could have been combined as a single comment to reduce typing, like this:

```
/* A small program to print a message to the screen
   Written by L. John Ribar. */
```

The following line:

```
#include <stdio.h>
```

tells the compiler to read the file **stdio.h** and to include its contents in the current file. **stdio.h** is a file known as a *header file*; it stores definitions used in many programs in one place so that they won't have to be retyped each time. Header files generally use the H filename extension. **stdio.h** contains the information about input and output functions and is included with all ANSI standard C compilers. Header files in C perform a similar function to FORTRAN FI and FD files.

The **< >** delimiters on the filename show that the file is a *system file*. System files come with the compiler and are stored in a special directory that the compiler knows about and can find. If quotation marks had been used instead, like this:

```
#include "stdio.h"
```

the compiler would have searched the current directory for the header file, instead of the system directory. Your own header files will generally be included by using the quotation mark (or local) version. FORTRAN Include files are generally found by looking along the path specified in the Include environment variable.

The following line is the start of the main program:

```
main()
```

As noted before, the **main()** function could have been declared with parameters. **main()** is a special function that allows you to either use or ignore the parameters. Functions other than **main()** either will always use parameters or will not have any parameters.

The next line has an opening curly brace:

```
{
```

This marks the beginning of the code of the **main()** function. Notice how both this brace and the one at the end of the program are in column 1, and that the code between them is indented.

This format is very common, but the C language has no restrictions on formatting—any columns can be used, and there is no need to specify continuation lines when they are needed. In fact, this entire program could have been entered like this:

```
/* A small C program to print a message to the screen.
Written by L. John Ribar. */
#include <stdio.h>
main(){printf("Hello again! \n");}
```

The only difference would be the readability of the program for anyone who needs to study it or make changes in the future. Formatting your code with future users in mind is important for both C-language and FORTRAN programming, but is not a requirement in either language. Because of this, you should set some goals for yourself regarding how your code should look; this will prevent confusion and save time for you or anyone else who has to come back to your code in the future.

This line:

```
printf("Hello again! \n");
```

contains a call to the function named **printf()**. In this case, a parameter—the string "Hello again! \n"—is sent into the function by placing it between the parentheses. **printf()** is a very common function, and is used in many C programs to output information to the screen, similar to the WRITE(*) function call in FORTRAN.

The \n at the end of the string is a shortcut notation for a carriage return, which makes the cursor move to the beginning of the next line on the screen after the string is printed. This is like pressing the carriage return on a typewriter after typing a line. This process is different in FORTRAN, where the default action is to start a new line, and suppression of the new line is accomplished with a $ specifier.

This ending curly brace:

```
}
```

marks the end of the **main()** function, and in this case, the end of the program.

Remember   Braces must always match up in C; each opening brace ({) requires a closing brace (}). If the compiler finds an uneven number of braces, it will flag it as an error, and you will need to find the missing, or extra, brace.

The Characters Used in C

The C language uses a standard set of characters. Numeric digits are used to represent numbers and alphabetic characters, digits and the underscore character are used in variable names. Any character can be part of a character string, and most mathematical functions are performed using the same characters that are used in FORTRAN.

Note   Unlike alphabetic characters used in FORTRAN, all characters are case-sensitive in C; therefore, the following variable names are all different:

myVariable
myvariable
MYVARIABLE

The following list of words are *reserved words* for the C language. They each have a special meaning within C, and the compiler will therefore not allow their use for naming variables or functions.

auto	double	int	struct
break	else	long	switch
case	enum	register	typedef
char	extern	return	union
const	float	short	unsigned
continue	for	signed	void
default	goto	sizeof	volatile
do	if	static	while

You should check your compiler manual, since other words may also be reserved by some compilers. For instance, many also reserve these words:

cdecl	fortran	near
far	huge	pascal

Special Characters

The following non-letter and non-digit characters are part of C. This list will act as a quick reference for you as you begin to read C language code; for more in-depth coverage of these concepts, look at one of the C books mentioned in the list at the front of this book.

Characters	Purpose
{ }	Delimit blocks of code.
( )	Delimit the parameter list in a function definition or a function call.
[ ]	Delimit the index of an array variable.
< >	Delimit the name of standard header files.
>	Indicates a greater-than comparison in equations.
<	Indicates a less-than comparison in equations.
==	Indicates an is-equal-to comparison in equations—this is often one of the things which takes a beginning C programmer longer to learn than anything else.
>=	Indicates greater-than or equal-to in equations.
<=	Indicates less-than or equal-to in equations.
!=	Indicates not-equal-to.
!	Indicates NOT—this negates the value of the item to its right.
~	Indicates the complement of a number.
/*	Begins a comment.
*/	Ends a comment.
' '	Delimit a single character.

Characters	Purpose
" "	Delimit a string of characters—also delimit the name of a local header file (instead of < and >).
*	Used in two ways: 1) As a multiplication symbol in equations. 2) To denote a pointer variable or the contents of a pointer variable.
+	Indicates addition in equations.
–	Indicates subtraction in equations.
/	Indicates division in equations.
%	Modulus symbol in equations—this is similar to division, but returns the remainder after dividing the two items.
+ +	Increments a number by 1.
– –	Decrements a number by 1.
|	ORs two numbers together at a binary level.
| |	ORs the Boolean value of two expressions together.
&	Used in two ways: 1) Denotes the address of the variable to its right. 2) ANDs two numbers together at a binary level.
&&	ANDs the Boolean value of two expressions together.
>>	Performs an arithmetic shift-right function.
<<	Performs an arithmetic shift-left function.
^	Performs a Binary Exclusive OR on two values.
?	In special C statements, determines which of two values to choose, based on a Boolean operation.
:	Used in conjunction with the ? operation.
#	Introduces a preprocessor directive.
\	Introduces a special character in a character constant or as part of a character string.
;	Ends every C statement.
=	Assigns values to a variable.
+=	Adds the value on the right to the variable on the left—combination of addition and assignment functions.

Characters	Purpose
-=	Subtracts the value on the right from the variable on the left—combination of subtraction and assignment functions.
*=	Multiplies the value on the right by the variable on the left—combination of multiplication and assignment functions.
/=	Divides the variable on the left by the value on the right—combination of division and assignment functions.
^=	Performs an exclusive OR on the value on the right and the variable on the left—combination of EOR and assignment functions.
&=	ANDs the value on the right and the variable on the left—combination of AND and assignment functions.

At this point, C might not look like it has many similarities with FORTRAN, but here are two programs, one in C and one in FORTRAN, that might help you start to tie them together. These programs both assign the variable **i** the value 1, and if **i** = 1, each prints "i is equal to 1". Here is the C program:

```
/* A C demo program */
/* By L. John Ribar, FORTRAN Programming for Windows */

#include <stdio.h>    /* include input/output routines */

main()
{
    int i;    /* declare an integer variable */
    i = 1;    /* assign a value of 1 to i */
    if (i==1) /* == is the equality comparison function */
        printf("i is equal to one \n");
    else
    {          /* { and } surround a block of code */
        printf("i is not equal to 1 \n");
        i = 1;
    }
}
```

Here is the FORTRAN program that does the same thing:

```
C A FORTRAN Demo Program
C By L. John Ribar, FORTRAN Programming for Windows

      PROGRAM ForDemo

      INTEGER i        ! Integer variable

      i = 1            ! Remember, case doesn't matter
      IF (i.EQ.1) THEN
         WRITE(*,*) ' i is equal to 1'
      ELSE
         WRITE(*,*) ' i is not equal to 1'
         i = 1
      END IF

      END              ! of the program
```

While these are trivial examples, and you may not understand everything that is going on in the C program, you may have started to see similarities.

 Remember Unlike many other programming languages, such as FORTRAN and Pascal, C is case-sensitive!

Writing Programs with Both C and FORTRAN

Historically, writing applications that use more than a single language has not been easy. Recently, compiler makers have been more cognizant of this, and have started generating more compatible object code. One of the greatest advances in this arena has been the introduction of DLLs, which allow applications to call for functions that might be created under any language.

In this section, you'll learn more about combining C and FORTRAN routines in a single application. Then you'll see how this interface is simplified when using DLLs. In both cases, however, there are specific topics in mixed-language programming that should be discussed.

The Basics of Mixed-Language Programming

Why would you want to mix routines from different languages in an application? There are many times when mixed-language programming can be a great time saver. For instance, a C program might need scientific calculations provided by a FORTRAN library. A FORTRAN programmer might want the user interface routines provided by a C language library.

In order to effectively utilize and create routines for mixed-language access, you must learn about naming conventions, function-calling conventions, and parameter-passing conventions for each of the languages involved.

Naming Conventions

When routines are called between multiple languages, care must be taken to account for differences in how each language stores variable and function names, the *naming conventions*. For instance, Microsoft FORTRAN stores all variable names in uppercase letters by default. This means that even if you name a variable LoopCount in your application, and FORTRAN is not case-sensitive, the name will be stored as LOOPCOUNT in the object file.

Microsoft C, on the other hand, stores all names as you name them, with case sensitivity. However, an underscore character (_) is attached to the front of the names you create. This means that if you have a variable called AverageValue, it will be stored in the object file as _AverageValue.

You might already see where naming conventions can cause problems in multi-language applications. If you have a FORTRAN variable called DotCount, and a C variable called DotCount, they would be stored as DOTCOUNT and _DotCount by the FORTRAN and C compilers, respectively.

 Note   You need to decide on one calling convention for your application. Then, either name all your FORTRAN variables with the C convention or name your C variables with the FORTRAN convention. If you do both, they won't match!

The naming convention is directly tied into the calling convention, discussed in the next section. When functions are called, their names must match between the calling routine and the called routine. Therefore, calling convention commands are used to equate names from different languages.

Calling Conventions

The *calling convention* used determines how a function will be called, and what naming convention will be used. This is managed in the prototype of C and the INTERFACE statement of FORTRAN.

To use the FORTRAN naming and calling conventions from your C programs, add the **fortran** keyword to your function names (for routines you write in C) and prototypes (for FORTRAN functions you wish to use from C). For instance, here is the prototype for the **julian()** function as it will be used from a C program:

```
extern double fortran julian(short *year,
                             short *month,
                             short *day);
```

In this prototype, **extern** denotes that the function resides in a different program module, **double** is the return value type (similar to REAL*8), and **fortran** denotes that FORTRAN naming and calling conventions will be used. The **short** parameters are the C type for INTEGER*2 variables.

From FORTRAN, if you wish to use a C language function with C naming and calling conventions, add [C] to your interface definition. The following example is the interface definition for a function in the FilesLib DLL that will be created later in this chapter.

```
INTERFACE TO SUBROUTINE TODAY [C,Alias:'_today']
+      ( MONTH, DAY, YEAR )
   INTEGER*2 MONTH [Reference]
   INTEGER*2 DAY   [Reference]
   INTEGER*2 YEAR  [Reference]
END
```

Here, the C conventions are specified, and the actual name of the routine in the C object code (**_today**) is specified as an alias. The actual name that will be found in the C file is actually **_today**, but from within the

FORTRAN application, you may call TODAY() as a subroutine. In this way, the differences in naming schemes can be nearly hidden from normal usage.

The calling convention also deals with the way in which parameters are passed between functions and which routine is responsible for adjusting the stack when the subroutine call returns to the calling procedure.

In FORTRAN, the parameters for the subroutine or function are pushed onto the stack from left to right. This means that the first parameter is pushed onto the stack first; then the second, the third, and so forth. Therefore, the last parameter passed into the function is the first one that can be pulled off of the stack. It is the responsibility of the called function to clear the stack when the function is complete.

In C, however, the parameters for the subroutine or function are pushed onto the stack from right to left. This means that the final parameter is pushed onto the stack first; then the second to the last, the third from the last, and so forth. The first parameter passed into the function is the first one that can be pulled off of the stack. It is the responsibility of the calling function to clear the stack when the function is complete.

Because of this arrangement, C can support functions with a varying number of parameters very simply—the first parameters just need to tell the system how many parameters will follow (FORTRAN also allows the VARYING parameter list, but it is not used by default).

Parameter-Passing Conventions

The naming and calling conventions discussed previously are relatively easy to manage. The more difficult convention to manage is the parameter-passing convention. The trouble here arises from the fact that different languages use different types of variables, and passing them is not always as straightforward as might be hoped.

Not all types of variables can be passed between C and FORTRAN. The following table lists the equivalent variable types, and their names in each of the two languages.

FORTRAN Variable Type	C Equivalent Type
INTEGER*2	short
INTEGER*4	long
REAL*4	float
REAL*8	double
CHARACTER*1	unsigned char

The FORTRAN LOGICAL*2 type can be replicated in C by creating a structure like this,

```
struct LOG2
{
   unsigned char value;
   unsigned char dummy;
};
```

in which **value** holds the logical value (1 means .TRUE., 0 means .FALSE.), and the dummy variable is not used. Likewise, LOGICAL*4 would be replicated as follows.

```
struct LOG4
{
   unsigned char value;
   unsigned char dummy[3];
};
```

Here, an array of three dummy values are used with the actual logical value to fill in the four bytes of the LOGICAL*4 variable.

Strings are a bit more difficult to manage. A FORTRAN string is simply a series of characters, the series being as long as the variable's definition. A C string, on the other hand, always ends with an ASCII value of 0. This marks the length of the string.

You can force FORTRAN to create a C-like string by following the string's definition with the letter C. You might recall that this trick was used in Chapter 3 to send C strings to Windows functions, with a procedure something like this:

```
C     Register the custom About box
      Status = AboutBoxQQ
   +         ('QW06 Test Program\r by John Ribar'C)
```

Without this capability, many C functions will not work correctly. All C string handling is based on the assumption that the strings will always end with an ASCII zero. In the sections that follow, you will see more examples of passing strings between FORTRAN and C.

BATCH File Diversion

Before getting into the actual process of building mixed-language applications under Windows, you might consider building DOS batch files (*.BAT) for some of the common compile and link routines you'll need. Here are a few that were used during the writing of this book; they are designed to be used with the Microsoft FORTRAN and C compilers.

Building a FORTRAN Application Using DLLs

The following batch file, BLDFOR.BAT, compiles the file named on the command line (do not use the FOR extension!) and then links the application. It assumes a DEF file with the same base name as the application.

```
REM BLDFOR.BAT - Build a FORTRAN Application that uses
REM                a Custom DEF file.
REM
REM First, compile the source file. /MW makes the
REM application QuickWin based.
FL /C /MW %1.FOR
REM
REM Now, link the application
LINK %1,,,/NOD LLIBFEW,%1
```

To use this batch file, assuming you had a source file named MYPROG.FOR, you would type

```
BLDFOR MYPROG
```

which would create an application called MYPROG.EXE.

Building a FORTRAN DLL

The next batch file, FORDLL.BAT, compiles the file named on the command line (do not use the FOR extension!), and then links it to build a dynamic link library. It assumes a DEF file with the same base name as the application, and a DLL file named similarly.

```
REM FORDLL.BAT - Build a FORTRAN DLL from a DEF file.
REM
REM First, compile the source file. /Aw tells compiler
REM not to assume where stack segment is located. /Gw
REM is used to generate the correct prologue and epilogue
REM code for a Windows-based DLL.
FL /C /Aw /Gw %1.FOR
REM
REM Now, create the library.
LINK %1,%1.DLL,,/NOD LDLLFEW,%1
```

To use this batch file, assuming you had a source file named MYFORLIB.FOR, you would type

```
FORDLL MYFORLIB
```

which would create a dynamic link library called MYFORLIB.DLL.

Building a C Application Using DLLs

The next batch file, BLDC.BAT, compiles the file named on the command line (do not use the C extension!) and then links the application. It assumes a DEF file with the same base name as the application.

```
REM BLDC.BAT - Build a C language application that uses
REM               a Custom DEF file.
REM
REM First, compile the source file. /Mq makes the
REM application QuickWin based. /AL uses the Large
REM memory model.
CL /c /AL /Mq %1.C
REM
REM Now, link the application
LINK %1,,,/NOD LLIBCEWQ LIBW,%1
```

To use this batch file, assuming you had a source file named MYCPROG.C, you would type

```
BLDC MYCPROG
```

which would create an application called MYCPROG.EXE.

Building a C DLL

The final batch file, CDLL.BAT, compiles the file named on the command line (do not use the C extension!) and then links the application. It assumes a DEF file with the same base name as the application.

```
REM CDLL.BAT - Build a C DLL from a custom DEF file.
REM
REM First, compile the source file. /Mq makes the
REM application QuickWin based. /AL uses the Large
REM memory model.
CL /c /AL /Mq %1.C
REM
REM Now, create the library.
LINK %1,%1.DLL,,/NOD LDLLCEW LIBW,%1
```

To use this batch file, assuming you had a source file named MYCLIB.FOR, you would type

```
CDLL MYCLIB
```

which would create a dynamic link library called MYCLIB.DLL.

Simplified Interfaces Using DLLs

The conventions that were discussed earlier make multi-language programming sometimes more difficult than it is worth. This is compounded when you are using two (or more!) compilers at the same time, different versions of the linker, libraries you have created and purchased from other vendors, and so on. The best way to manage all the many files is by using a makefile, which is fed into Microsoft's NMAKE or WATCOM's MAKE utility to perform all the necessary functions.

To simplify your programming, you might wish to place all of your functions into dynamic link libraries. Numerous advantages using DLLs were detailed in Chapter 5. One additional advantage is that you do not need to directly link with each of these libraries as you create your applications—linking will be taken care of by Windows when the application is run. This will simplify the building of applications. Remember, however, that the conventions of naming, parameter passing, and function calling must still be followed.

In the rest of this chapter, the Julian date DLL (created in Chapter 5) will be used, as well as a FilesLib DLL, which will be created shortly. Once you understand how these applications are built, you can enhance their functionality with your own FORTRAN functions and libraries.

Calling FORTRAN Functions from C

The first thing you need to do is to call the Julian library from a simple C program. This is probably the simplest of the interfaces that can be performed between C and FORTRAN, based on the fact that the parameters and return value for the Julian function are all fixed sizes. Passing strings is a bit more tricky, and will be covered in the next section, when the FilesLib library is created.

In order for a C program to use a FORTRAN function, a *prototype* for that function must be created. A prototype in C is similar to a FORTRAN INTERFACE statement, in that it describes the interface that will be used to call the function. The prototype for calling the Julian library will look like this:

```
extern double fortran julian( short *year,
                              short *month,
                              short *day);
```

This prototype declares that the **julian()** function will return a **double** value (equivalent to FORTRAN REAL*8) and will take three **short** (INTEGER*2) parameters, by reference. The FORTRAN calling convention will be used (**fortran**), and the function resides externally to the C application (**extern**).

The FORTRAN default is to pass all parameters by reference. This means that the address of the parameter is actually passed, so the function or subroutine can make changes to that variable if necessary. The C standard is to pass all variables by value, meaning that only a copy of the value is passed, and that the original variable cannot be changed.

Now that the prototype is defined, a C program can be written to take advantage of the library. The following program, written in C, calls **julian()** twice, to determine the age, or duration, between two dates.

```
/*
   CJulian.C

   C Program to call a FORTRAN DLL
   By L. John Ribar

   System:   Microsoft FORTRAN and C
   Date:     10 Oct 1994
   OS:       Microsoft Windows
*/

#include <stdio.h>

/* Prototypes */
extern double fortran julian( short *year,
                             short *month, short *day);

void main()
{
/*
   This test program will determine the age of a
   person born on May 10, 1961, as of the date
   October 10, 1994.
*/
   short m1 = 5, m2 = 10;
   short d1 = 10, d2 = 10;
   short y1 = 61, y2 = 94;
   double j1, j2;

   printf("Julian of the first date is %7.0lf\n",
       j1=julian( &y1, &m1, &d1 ) );
   printf("Julian of the second date is %7.0lf\n",
       j2=julian( &y2, &m2, &d2 ) );
   printf("The age of the person is %d days or %d years\n",
       (int) (j2-j1), (int) (j2-j1)/365 );
}
```

To compile and link this application, you need to create a FORTRAN DEFinition file, to allow the program to take advantage of the Julian DLL file. The DEF file, in this case, would look like this:

```
; CJulian.DEF
; This is a linker definition file for the Julian date
;      test program in C
; By John Ribar  -  21 Sept 1994  -  Microsoft C 7.0

NAME          CJulian
DESCRIPTION   'Julian Dates Tester in C'
EXETYPE       WINDOWS 3.0
STUB          'WINSTUB.EXE'

CODE          PRELOAD MOVEABLE DISCARDABLE
DATA          PRELOAD MOVEABLE SINGLE
HEAPSIZE      1024
STACKSIZE     5120
IMPORTS       JULIAN.Julian
```

This DEF file is straightforward, as discussed in Chapter 5. The only customization needed was to add the IMPORTS statement to allow the use of the Julian function from the JULIAN DLL file.

To compile CJulian.C, use the following command:

```
CL /c /AL /Mq CJulian.C
```

To link it, use

```
LINK CJulian,,,/NOD LLIBCEW LIBW,CJulian
```

To simplify remembering these commands, you might want to use the BLDC batch file developed earlier in this chapter, and type

```
BLDC CJulian
```

to both compile and link the application.

Again, this is a simple interface because both C and FORTRAN manage numbers the same way, as long as compatible numeric types are selected. In the next section, you will see what happens when strings are passed between the languages.

Calling C Functions from FORTRAN

There might be many times when you will want to call C functions from your FORTRAN applications. There are a great many C functions not available in the Microsoft FORTRAN libraries, so using the C equivalents, rather than rewriting the functions from scratch, makes sense.

As an example, here is a C function that gets the current date from the system clock:

```
/*
   today() is a function that returns the current date
   information.
*/
void today( short *m, short *d, short *y )
{
   /* this structure is used to receive information
      from the DOS function call that follows */
   struct dosdate_t todayInfo;

   _dos_getdate( &todayInfo );

   /* now, pull out the values to pass back */
   *m = (short) todayInfo.month;
   *d = (short) todayInfo.day;
   *y = (short) todayInfo.year;
}
```

To use this function from FORTRAN, just create an INTERFACE declaration, like this:

```
      INTERFACE TO SUBROUTINE TODAY [C,Alias:'_today']
   +       ( MONTH, DAY, YEAR )
      INTEGER*2 MONTH [Reference]
      INTEGER*2 DAY   [Reference]
      INTEGER*2 YEAR  [Reference]
   END
```

You might wonder why the variables are marked [Reference], when FORTRAN already passes variables by reference. Very simply, since the subroutine is marked with [C] and the C default is passing variables by value, the variables in this call have to be specifically marked as being passed by reference.

This may seem a little inside out, but with practice you'll be fine. One way to handle multi-language programming is to always specify variables as being passed by reference or by value, even if it is the default. Then you'll always know which method is being used.

Before creating an entire application, a few additional functions are necessary in this C language DLL. These C functions, called **firstfile()** and **nextfile()**, are used to list all the files that DOS can find in the current directory.

First, a C header file is created. This will be used to document the interfaces to the functions; it will be named **files.h**. Here is the listing of that file:

```
/*
    Files.H - Header file for functions that implement
    the listing files for C and FORTRAN applications.

    Author:     L. John Ribar
    System:     Microsoft C 7.0
    Date:       11 Oct 1994
    OS:         DOS and Windows
*/

/* data types */

struct c_date
{
    short day;
    short month;
    short year;
};

/* prototypes */

/*
    firstfile() is used to start selection of a group of
    filenames. The dirname parameter specifies the file
    name that is requested. filetype designates the types
    of files that should be selected (see text).

    The return value is true (1) if a file was found; else
    it is false (0).
*/
short firstfile( const char *dirname,    /* requested files */
                 char filetype,          /* file types */
```

```
                    char *filename,         /* file found */
                    long *size,             /* file size */
                    struct c_date *filedate );/* file date */

/*
   nextfile() is used to select the next file in a series
   started by firstfile().

   The return value is true (1) if a file was found; else
   it is false (0).
*/
short nextfile(  char *filename,         /* file found */
                    long *size,             /* file size */
                    struct c_date *filedate );/* file date */

/*
   today() is a function that returns the current date
   information.
*/
void today( short *m, short *d, short *y );

/* end of files.h */
```

To be able to call these functions from FORTRAN, you should also create a FORTRAN interface file, perhaps called FILES.FI, which will look like this:

```
!
!   Files.FI - FORTRAN File Library Interfaces
!
!   Author:    L. John Ribar
!   System:    Microsoft FORTRAN 5.1, C 7.0
!   Date:      13 Oct 1994
!   OS:        Microsoft Windows
!

!   FIRSTFILE() is used to start selection of a group of
!   filenames. The DIRNAME parameter specifies the file
!   name that is requested. FILETYPE designates the types
!   of files that should be selected (see text).

!   The return value is true (1) if a file was found; else
!   it is false (0).

     INTERFACE TO INTEGER*2 FUNCTION
   +        FIRSTFILE [C,Alias:'_firstfile']
```

```
     +          ( DIRNAME, FILEATTR, FILENAME, FILESIZE,
     +            FILEDATE )
        CHARACTER*12  DIRNAME   [Reference]
        CHARACTER*1   FILEATTR
        CHARACTER*12  FILENAME  [Reference]
        INTEGER*4     FILESIZE  [Reference]
        STRUCTURE /CDATE/
            INTEGER*2 MONTH
            INTEGER*2 DAY
            INTEGER*2 YEAR
        END STRUCTURE
        RECORD /CDATE/ FILEDATE [Reference]
     END

!    NEXTFILE() is used to select the next file in a series
!    started by FIRSTFILE().

!    The return value is true (1) if a file was found; else
!    it is false (0).

     INTERFACE TO INTEGER*2 FUNCTION
     +       NEXTFILE [C,Alias:'_nextfile']
     +          ( FILENAME, FILESIZE, FILEDATE )
        CHARACTER*12  FILENAME  [Reference]
        INTEGER*4     FILESIZE  [Reference]
        STRUCTURE /CDATE/
            INTEGER*2 MONTH
            INTEGER*2 DAY
            INTEGER*2 YEAR
        END STRUCTURE
        RECORD /CDATE/ FILEDATE [Reference]
     END

!    TODAY() is a subroutine that returns the current date
!    information.

     INTERFACE TO SUBROUTINE TODAY [C,Alias:'_today']
     +       ( MONTH, DAY, YEAR )
        INTEGER*2 MONTH [Reference]
        INTEGER*2 DAY   [Reference]
        INTEGER*2 YEAR  [Reference]
     END
```

Notice that all the functions are marked as following the C conventions (using [C]), and that the variables are marked as being passed by reference.

Now, the actual functions are written in the C source file called
FILESLIB.C, which is shown here:

```
/*
    FILESLIB.C - A C Library of functions that implement
    the listing of files for C and FORTRAN applications.

    Author:    L. John Ribar
    System:    Microsoft C 7.0
    Date:      11 Oct 1994
    OS:        DOS and Windows
*/

#include "files.h"    /* prototypes */
#include <dos.h>      /* system files */
#include <errno.h>
#include <string.h>

static struct find_t fileInfo;

/*
    firstfile() is used to start selection of a group of
    filenames. The dirname parameter specifies the file
    name that is requested. filetype designates the types
    of files that should be selected (see text).

    The return value is true (1) if a file was found; else
    it is false (0).
*/
short firstfile( const char *dirname,    /* requested files */
                 char filetype,          /* file types */
                 char *filename,         /* file found */
                 long *size,             /* file size */
                 struct c_date *filedate ) /* file date */
{
    int result;

    result = _dos_findfirst( dirname, (unsigned) filetype,
                             &fileInfo );
    if (result != 0)
        return 0;

    strcpy( filename, fileInfo.name );
    *size = fileInfo.size;

    /* The DOS date information is stored in a single word
```

```
            (16 bits) to conserve space. Here, break out the date
            based on the bits that each portion consumes. */

        /* For day, just mask off bits 0 through 4 */
        filedate->day=fileInfo.wr_date & 0x001f; /* bits 0-4 */

        /* For month, mask bits 5 through 8, and divide by 32
           ( 2 to the 5th power ) */
        filedate->month=(fileInfo.wr_date & 0x01e0) / 32; /*5-8*/

        /* For the year, mask off bits 9 through 15, and divide
           by 512 (2 to the 9th power) */
        filedate->year=(fileInfo.wr_date & 0xfe00) / 512; /*9-15*/

        return 1;
}


/*
    nextfile() is used to select the next file in a series
    started by firstfile().

    The return value is true (1) if a file was found; else
    it is false (0).
*/
short nextfile(  char *filename,          /* file found */
                 long *size,              /* file size */
                 struct c_date *filedate ) /* file date */
{
    int result;

    result = _dos_findnext( &fileInfo );
    if (result != 0)
        return 0;

    strcpy( filename, fileInfo.name );
    *size = fileInfo.size;

    /* Break out the DOS date information, as documented in
       FirstFile() */
    filedate->day=fileInfo.wr_date & 0x001f; /* bits 0-4 */
    filedate->month=(fileInfo.wr_date & 0x01e0) / 32; /*5-8*/
    filedate->year=(fileInfo.wr_date & 0xfe00) / 512; /*9-15*/

    return 1;
}

/*
```

```
      today() is a function that returns the current date
      information.
*/
void today( short *m, short *d, short *y )
{
    struct dosdate_t todayInfo;

    _dos_getdate( &todayInfo );
    *m = (short) todayInfo.month;
    *d = (short) todayInfo.day;
    *y = (short) todayInfo.year;
}
```

The DLL is created from this source file using the following steps. If you don't remember all the details of building a DLL, you might want to run through Chapter 5 again.

First, a DEFinition file is created, which specifies that a DLL is being built, and which routines are being exported. The DEF file for a C DLL is only slightly different from that for a FORTRAN DLL, as you'll see here:

```
; FilesLib.DEF
; This is a linker definition file for the file-handling DLL
; By John Ribar  -  21 Sept 1994  -  Microsoft C 7.0

LIBRARY        FilesLib.DLL
DESCRIPTION    'DLL for File Lists'
EXETYPE        WINDOWS 3.0
CODE           PRELOAD MOVEABLE DISCARDABLE
DATA           PRELOAD MOVEABLE
HEAPSIZE       1024

; Export the function requirements
EXPORTS
     _firstfile
     _nextfile
     _today
     WEP @1 RESIDENTNAME

SEGMENTS 'WEP_TEXT' FIXED PRELOAD
```

 Note The C functions are shown with their full object filenames, including the leading underscore characters. This is to demonstrate that the actual names of the functions have to be listed in the EXPORTS statement.

Once the DEF file is created, you are ready to compile and link the DLL using the following two commands:

```
cl /c /AL /Mq FILESLIB.C
link FILESLIB,FILESLIB.DLL,,/NOD LIBW LDLLCEW,FILESLIB
```

Alternately, you can use the CDLL batch file created earlier in this chapter and just type

```
CDLL FILESLIB
```

This will perform the compilation and the link steps that are necessary.

Once the DLL is built, make sure to copy it to your Windows directory (where your JULIAN DLL file should also be) so that any Windows applications will have access to the functions.

The next step in this development effort is to create an application or two that make use of the DLLs that have been constructed. Here is a simple C program that uses the FILESLIB DLL to list all of the files in the current directory.

```
/*
    Files.C - A C Program that uses a C DLL

    Author:    L. John Ribar
    System:    Microsoft C 7.0
    Date:      11 Oct 1994
    OS:        DOS and Windows
*/

#include "files.h"    /* prototypes */
#include <dos.h>       /* system files */
#include <errno.h>
#include <string.h>

void main( int argc, char *argv[] )
{
    int res;                  /* result of function calls */
    char filename[15];        /* filename found */
    struct c_date filedate;   /* file date found */
    long filesize;            /* size of file found */
    long totalsize = 0L;      /* size of all files */
    int count = 0;            /* number of files found */
    short day, month, year;   /* today's date */
```

```
/* Get today's Date */
today( &month, &day, &year );

/* Normalize the year */
year -= 1900;

/* Now display today's date */
printf("Today is %02d/%02d/%02d\n",
   month, day, year);

/* If there is a command-line argument, use that to
   start the file listing, otherwise show all files. */
if (argc < 2)
   res = firstfile( "*.*", _A_NORMAL, filename, &filesize,
      &filedate );
else
   res = firstfile( argv[1], _A_NORMAL, filename, &filesize,
      &filedate );

/* As long as files are found, keep looping */
while (res == 1 )
{
   /* Display the file's information, including age */
   printf("%12s %10ld %02d/%02d/%02d \n",
      filename, filesize, (int) filedate.month,
      (int) filedate.day, (int)filedate.year%100);

   /* Increment the count and total bytes */
   count++;
   totalsize += filesize;

   /* Try to read another file */
   res = nextfile( filename, &filesize, &filedate );
}

/* Now display the totals calculated */
printf("Total of %d files, %ld bytes\n", count,
   totalsize );
}
```

The preceding program, called FILES.C, shows the files in the current directory. If you pass a parameter, it will be used as the criterion for the files to be listed. If no parameter is used, all files will be listed. You can run the program with this command:

```
FILES *.C
```

To build this program, you need a DEF file for FILES.C that allows the use of the FILESDEF DLL. It can be as simple as this:

```
; Files.DEF - Definition file allowing use of
;             FILESLIB DLL   C

NAME            Files,WINDOWAPI
EXETYPE         WINDOWS 3.0
PROTMODE
CODE            PRELOAD MOVEABLE DISCARDABLE
DATA            PRELOAD MOVEABLE
HEAPSIZE        1024
STACKSIZE       8096

; Import the DLL requirements
IMPORTS
    FILESLIB._firstfile
    FILESLIB._nextfile
    FILESLIB._today
```

Note The C functions are shown with their full object filenames, including the leading underscore characters. This is to demonstrate that the actual name of the function must be listed in the IMPORTS statement.

To compile and link the FILES program, use the BLDC batch file created earlier. Your command line will look like this:

```
BLDC Files
```

This command will create an executable file called FILES.EXE, which can be run from the Windows Program Manager or File Manager.

Now is the moment you've been waiting for. The next two programs are complete examples of programs using C and FORTRAN DLLs. One application uses a main program written in C, and the other uses a main routine written in FORTRAN.

Calling FORTRAN and C DLLs from Applications

In the vein of the previous example, you might want to provide your file listing program with access to the Julian DLL. This will allow the program to show the age of each file, which will be helpful when you need to clean old files off your disk.

First, you will see how this is done in C, since the interface is more direct. Then, a second version of the application will be built, with similar features, implemented as a FORTRAN program.

To create a C program that uses the FORTRAN Julian date DLL, simply add the required new functions to the previous example. Here, you might wish to show the age of each file, as shown here:

```
/*
    Files2.C - A C Program that uses both C and FORTRAN DLLs.

    Author:    L. John Ribar
    System:    Microsoft C 7.0
    Date:      11 Oct 1994
    OS:        DOS and Windows
*/

#include "files.h"    /* prototypes */
#include <dos.h>      /* system files */
#include <errno.h>
#include <string.h>

/* Prototypes */
extern double fortran julian( short *year,
                              short *month, short *day);


void main( int argc, char *argv[] )
{
    int res;                    /* result of function calls */
    char filename[15];          /* filename found */
```

```
struct c_date filedate;    /* file date found */
long filesize;             /* size of file found */
long totalsize = 0L;       /* size of all files */
int count = 0;             /* number of files found */
short day, month, year;    /* today's date */
double todayJ, fJulian;    /* Julian dates */
short fDay, fMonth, fYear; /* file date, in 3 pieces */

/* Get today's Date */
today( &month, &day, &year );

/* Normalize the year */
year -= 1900;

/* Now display today's date */
printf("Today is %02d/%02d/%02d\n",
    month, day, year);

/* Calculate today's Julian date */
todayJ = julian( &year, &month, &day );

/* If there is a command-line argument, use that to
   start the file listing, otherwise show all files. */
if (argc < 2)
    res = firstfile( "*.*", _A_NORMAL, filename, &filesize,
        &filedate );
else
    res = firstfile( argv[1], _A_NORMAL, filename, &filesize,
        &filedate );

/* As long as files are found, keep looping */
while (res == 1 )
{
    /* Pull out file dates for Julian calculation */
    fMonth = filedate.month;
    fDay = filedate.day;
    filedate.year += 80;  /* dates are based on 1980 */
    fYear = filedate.year;

    /* Determine the file's Julian date */
    fJulian = julian( &fYear, &fMonth, &fDay );

    /* Display the file's information, including age */
    printf("%12s %10ld %02d/%02d/%02d ",
        filename, filesize, (int) filedate.month,
        (int) filedate.day, (int)filedate.year%100);
    printf("  Age (days): %4d\n",
```

```
                    (int) (todayJ - fJulian) );

        /* Increment the count and total bytes */
        count++;
        totalsize += filesize;

        /* Try to read another file */
        res = nextfile( filename, &filesize, &filedate );
    }

    /* Now display the totals calculated */
    printf("Total of %d files, %ld bytes\n", count,
        totalsize );
}
```

Because of the similarity to the previous program, the FILES2 DEF file only requires the addition of an IMPORTS statement for the Julian function:

```
; FILES2.DEF - Definition file allowing use of
;              Julian DLL - FORTRAN, and
;              FilesLib DLL - C

NAME            Files2,WINDOWAPI
EXETYPE         WINDOWS 3.0
PROTMODE
CODE            PRELOAD MOVEABLE DISCARDABLE
DATA            PRELOAD MOVEABLE
HEAPSIZE        1024
STACKSIZE       8096

; Import the DLL requirements
IMPORTS
    JULIAN.Julian
    FILESLIB._firstfile
    FILESLIB._nextfile
    FILESLIB._today
```

Using the batch files from this chapter, building this file becomes as simple as

```
BLDC Files2
```

Creating a FORTRAN front end for these DLLs takes a bit more work. First, interfaces to the DLLs must be created. This is not too important

with the FORTRAN Julian DLL, but for the C-based FILESLIB DLL, the
following interfaces are required and are stored in the file FILES.FI:

```
!
!     FILES.FI - FORTRAN File Library Interfaces
!
!     Author:    L. John Ribar
!     System:    Microsoft FORTRAN 5.1, C 7.0
!     Date:      13 Oct 1994
!     OS:        Microsoft Windows
!

!     FIRSTFILE() is used to start selection of a group of
!     filenames. The DIRNAME parameter specifies the file
!     name that is requested. FILETYPE designates the types
!     of files that should be selected (see text).

!     The return value is true (1) if a file was found; else
!     it is false (0).

      INTERFACE TO INTEGER*2 FUNCTION
     +      FIRSTFILE [C,Alias:'_firstfile']
     +      ( DIRNAME, FILEATTR, FILENAME, FILESIZE,
     +      FILEDATE )
      CHARACTER*12  DIRNAME   [Reference]
      CHARACTER*1   FILEATTR
      CHARACTER*12  FILENAME  [Reference]
      INTEGER*4     FILESIZE  [Reference]
      STRUCTURE /CDATE/
          INTEGER*2 MONTH
          INTEGER*2 DAY
          INTEGER*2 YEAR
      END STRUCTURE
      RECORD /CDATE/ FILEDATE [Reference]
      END

!     NEXTFILE() is used to select the next file in a series
!     started by FIRSTFILE().

!     The return value is true (1) if a file was found; else
!     it is false (0).

      INTERFACE TO INTEGER*2 FUNCTION
     +      NEXTFILE [C,Alias:'_nextfile']
     +      ( FILENAME, FILESIZE, FILEDATE )
      CHARACTER*12  FILENAME  [Reference]
```

```
      INTEGER*4      FILESIZE [Reference]
      STRUCTURE /CDATE/
         INTEGER*2 MONTH
         INTEGER*2 DAY
         INTEGER*2 YEAR
      END STRUCTURE
      RECORD /CDATE/ FILEDATE [Reference]
   END

!   TODAY() is a subroutine that returns the current date
!   information.

   INTERFACE TO SUBROUTINE TODAY [C,Alias:'_today']
  +      ( MONTH, DAY, YEAR )
      INTEGER*2 MONTH [Reference]
      INTEGER*2 DAY   [Reference]
      INTEGER*2 YEAR  [Reference]
   END
```

Most of the interface information is fairly straightforward, or has been covered in detail already. But one thing bears additional study: the passing of strings between C and FORTRAN.

In the C language, a parameter designated as **char *** is a string of undetermined length. As mentioned earlier in this chapter, C handles strings knowing that the last character is always an ASCII 0, so no length information is needed.

FORTRAN, however, only allows strings of fixed lengths. Therefore, in the example above, the INTERFACE statements for FIRSTFILE() and NEXTFILE() include fixed-length strings. Fixed lengths allow the FORTRAN compiler to determine the length of each of the strings. A length of 12 characters was chosen because it is the longest filename allowed by DOS (an eight-character name, a period, and a three-character extension).

The actual FORTRAN program looks vaguely reminiscent of the FILES2 program:

```
!
!   FFILES.FOR - FORTRAN File Lister, using both C and
!               FORTRAN code in a cooperative way.
!
!   Author:   L. John Ribar
!   System:   Microsoft FORTRAN 5.1, C 7.0
!   Date:     13 Oct 1994
!   OS:       Microsoft Windows
```

```
!

            INCLUDE 'FILES.FI'

            PROGRAM FFiles

            INTEGER*2    tMonth, tDay, tYear
            INTEGER*2    status, myAttr
            CHARACTER*1  myChar
            CHARACTER*13 myFile, dirName
            INTEGER*4    mySize
            INTEGER*2    FirstFile, NextFile
            REAL*8       Julian, todayJ, fileJ

!    This structure replicates the one shown in the
!    interfaces for FIRSTFILE() and NEXTFILE(), and
!    is used to declare local variables of the same
!    type.
            STRUCTURE /CDATE/
               INTEGER*2 MONTH
               INTEGER*2 DAY
               INTEGER*2 YEAR
            END STRUCTURE

            RECORD /CDATE/ myDate

!    Get today's date and display it
            CALL today( tMonth, tDay, tYear )
            tYear = tYear - 1900    ! Normalize to 2 digits
            WRITE(*,100) tMonth, tDay, tYear
100         FORMAT(' Today is ',I2,'/',I2,'/',I2)

!    Determine today's Julian date
            todayJ = Julian( tYear, tMonth, tDay )

!    Start searching for files
            dirName = '*.*'C         ! Use C format string
            myAttr = 0               ! Search for all file types
            myChar = CHAR(myAttr)
            status = FirstFile( dirName, myChar, myFile,
          +   mySize, myDate )

150         CONTINUE
!    As long as there are files found, continue
            IF (status.NE.1) GOTO 200

!    File dates are offset from 1980, so add 80 here
```

```
      myDate.Year = myDate.Year + 80
      fileJ = Julian( myDate.Year, myDate.Month,
   +     myDate.Day)

!     Display the file's information, including age
      WRITE(*,160) myFile, mySize, INT(todayJ-fileJ)
160   FORMAT(' ',A12,' ',I8,' bytes. Age(days): ',I4)

!     Go for another file
      status = NextFile( myFile, mySize, myDate )
      GOTO 150

200   CONTINUE
      END
```

Again, due to the batch files created earlier, building this application involves the following command:

```
BLDFOR FFiles
```

The application also uses the following DEFinition file:

```
; FFILES.DEF - Definition file allowing use of
;              Julian DLL - FORTRAN, and
;              FilesLib DLL - C

NAME           Files,WINDOWAPI
EXETYPE        WINDOWS 3.0
PROTMODE
CODE           PRELOAD MOVEABLE DISCARDABLE
DATA           PRELOAD MOVEABLE
HEAPSIZE       1024
STACKSIZE      8096

; Import the DLL requirements
IMPORTS
    JULIAN.Julian
    FILESLIB._firstfile
    FILESLIB._nextfile
    FILESLIB._today
```

You might notice how similar this file is to the DEF file used for the C version of this application.

Using Other Front Ends

In this chapter, you have been introduced to the sometimes difficult task of mixed-language programming. Now that you know the difficult parts, you should learn about the fun parts. In the next chapter, you'll learn how to create very user-oriented front ends for your function libraries. Since you are already familiar with language interfacing conventions, Chapter 7 can give you more of an *artistic* introduction to Windows programming!

CHAPTER

Using Visual Basic as a Front-End Generator

*I*n the previous chapter, you saw how the C language can be used with FORTRAN functions to create Windows applications. While combining the two languages offers a great deal of flexibility, using them together to build user interfaces is still not easy. In this chapter, you will see how Visual Basic, with its forms-based paradigm, can be used to build front ends quickly for your FORTRAN routines.

The Essentials of Visual Basic

Earlier in this book, you were introduced to the concept that "pure" Windows programming is quite different from any FORTRAN programming you have done previously. The biggest reason for this difference is the multiplicity of input that can be provided to your Windows applications. Not only can input be entered from the keyboard, but the mouse, menus, buttons, and other sources continuously flood data into your programs.

One exciting tool to help you ease into this new paradigm of programming is Microsoft Visual Basic, or VB. VB, while inheriting the BASIC name (Beginner's All-purpose Symbolic Instruction Code), has gone beyond any other current development environment for the creation of user-based Windows applications. The two major purposes for this are the forms-based front-end designer and the simplicity of the Visual Basic code actually used.

Forms and Attributes

Visual Basic helps you overcome the hurdle of Windows programming by approaching the development cycle in an entirely new way. In FORTRAN, you often design the code for your application and then add a user interface at the end, be that interface simple or complicated.

Under VB, you first design the user interface: the windows, dialog boxes, and menus that will be seen by the user when your program is run. Then you add code to each of the items, specifying what should happen when each item is selected.

For instance, if you want to create a menu displaying the items File, Edit, and Quit, you just use the VB menu editor, place three items into a menu, and tell VB what to do when each item is picked from the menu.

When you start VB, you are greeted with the design mode screen, which looks like Figure 7-1.

Near the center of the screen is the first form of your application. This form is where you will create the look of your program, adding a menu, text, input fields, and other objects to increase the usability of your application.

To the left side of the screen is the icon bar menu, which presents several design tools for use on the current form. These are tools that allow you to add specific features to your forms. They include text (for viewing only); text that can be edited or entered; buttons (which can be pressed to make events happen); pictures (including bitmap and icon images); radio and check buttons; scroll bars; combo boxes; timers; and drive, directory, and file list objects. The more common features, shown at the top of the icon bar menu, are described here. Additional buttons and associated features are available from a multitude of other software vendors.

FIGURE
7-1

The Visual Basic design mode screen

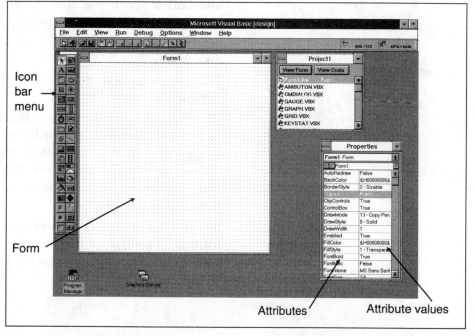

Icon/Feature	Purpose
Pointer	Points to objects so that they can be moved or deleted, or can have their attributes changed.
Labels	Places text on the form. Labels cannot be changed by the user. Your program, however, can change the text and attributes associated with a label.
Group	Groups items together visually on a form. This feature helps users understand that certain items should be considered together.
Check Box	Allows the user to turn an option on and off. Your application can handle these changes automatically.
Combo Box	This is a text box combined with a list box. It allows the user to either type in an answer or select one from a list.
Horizontal Scroll Bar	Allows the user to scroll through a picture or through a section of text that is larger than the form or the object to which it is attached.
Timer	This tool can be used to automatically run a subroutine at a preset time interval.
File Folder	Allows the user to select a directory from the directory structure in place of the current disk drive.
Letter	This tool is used to display the list of files in the current directory.
Disk Drive	Allows selection of the default disk drive. This tool can be used with the File folder and Letter to give the user full selection access to all drives, directories, and files on the computer; you can accomplish this with less than a dozen lines of code.
Vertical Scroll Bar	Allows the user to scroll through a picture or through a section of text that is larger than the form or the object to which it is attached.

Icon/Feature	Purpose
List Box	Presents a list of items from which the user may choose.
Radio Button	This type of button is selected in a group. In a group of radio buttons, only one button may be selected at a time. These are different from check boxes, which can be checked or unchecked independently of the others.
Pushbutton	Allows the user to signal that an event should take place.
Text Entry	These tools are used for gathering user input from the form. All input is retrieved as text, so the text must be converted to a number using VAL() if calculations are to be done.
Picture	Lets you place pictures or icons in your forms. For instance, in Figure 7-3, you can see a Notepad icon near the bottom of the frame. If you write a subroutine for the clicking action on this icon, the About box can be displayed with little effort just by clicking the mouse on the icon when the application runs.

As you click each item with your mouse, a new instance, or copy, of that object is taken to the form currently being created. Once the item exists on the form, you can move, size, and place the item with your mouse. You can also change the attributes of each item, as will be discussed later.

As you are building forms, a list of all the forms that have already been created will be kept in a window at the right side of the screen. If you click on any of the forms listed, VB will immediately bring that form to the "top of the stack" so that it can be viewed or managed.

As objects are placed on the form, they can be manipulated through the use of their attributes. Each type of object, including the form itself, has specific types of attributes; many of them are similar for most (or all) of the objects, such as the following:

Attribute	Purpose
BackColor	Sets the background color of the object or form.
Caption	Names most non-editable objects.
ControlBox	Determines whether the Control Box icon will be shown in the resulting window.
FontSize	Specifies the size of the font that will be displayed.
FontName	Designates the typeface of the text that will be displayed.
ForeColor	Sets the foreground color of the object or form.
FormName	Indicates the name that will replace the default name (Form1, Form2, etc.) as the name of the form.
Icon	Indicates the name of the icon that should be shown when the current form is minimized.
MaxButton	Creates a Maximize button on the form.
MinButton	Creates a Minimize button on the form.
Picture	Adds a picture to a form or imports a picture to be used as the background for the entire form.
Text	For input objects, holds the information entered by the user.

As objects are added to each form, their attributes are shown in the design window, just below the Visual Basic menu bar. You will see the attributes listed at the left edge of the window, with the current value of each attribute shown directly to its right.

As you create your application, you might design additional forms, which are tied together through a menu or through actual BASIC program code. A menu can be added to any form. Figure 7-2 shows a menu (for the Julian date calculator) that will be built as this chapter progresses.

Designing the Julian Date Manager application

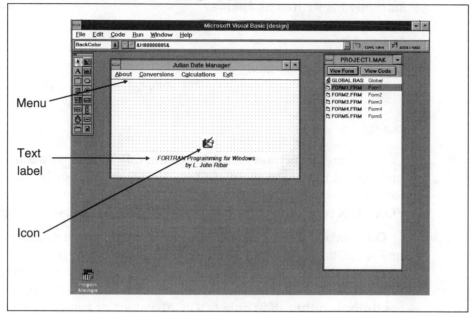

Menu

Text
label

Icon

Writing Code

There are many similarities between FORTRAN code and Visual Basic code, including the following:

□ Both FORTRAN and VB are case-*in*sensitive. This means that variable names do not care about the case of each letter. Case-insensitivity is good because there is less chance of a typing error; however, it does restrict the number and variety of names that can be created.

□ Both FORTRAN and VB have the concepts of functions and subroutines. A function is a piece of code that returns a value when it completes execution. A subroutine, on the other hand, does not return a value. The CALL keyword is used to call a subroutine.

Other types of statements in VB are similar to FORTRAN. A VB If statement is written as follows:

```
If condition Then
   statements1
Else If condition Then
   statements2
Else
   statements3
End If
```

There are numerous examples of the differences between FORTRAN and Visual Basic—so many, in fact, that they will not be covered here. Realize, however, that given all the front ends you can put on your FORTRAN code, an environment like VB is a great place to start.

One major change from FORTRAN is that VB treats numbers as TRUE or FALSE based upon their value. This is similar to the system used in C, except that in VB, 0 is considered FALSE and –1 is considered TRUE. What this all means is that an IF statement can use numbers in the conditions, rather than only LOGICAL values or comparisons.

Another slight change from FORTRAN is the For-Next loop that VB uses as a replacement for the **DO** loop. The following two loops will perform similar functions:

```
!    FORTRAN loop to add some numbers
DO I=1,10
   J = J + I*I
END DO


'  Visual Basic FOR loop to add numbers
For I = 1 to 10
   J = J + I*I
Next I
```

Note As you can see in this example, the VB comment starts with a single quotation mark. A VB comment can start anywhere in a line of code; it extends to the end of that line.

The actual coding requirements are reduced immensely with a VB front end for your FORTRAN libraries. You only write code for performing specific functions—no code is written to control user-interface! Later in this chapter, an entire application will be built, and you will see how simple VB code can be.

Calling FORTRAN Routines from a VB Application

Visual Basic uses the same calling and naming conventions as FOR-TRAN. (For a review of these concepts, see Chapter 6.) This means that very little work needs to be done for your FORTRAN functions to be actually used from within VB applications.

There are two keys to the interface: using compatible variable types, and writing VB interface statements to call FORTRAN routines in Dynamic Link Libraries.

VB Variable Types

Visual Basic has six standard variable types. Unlike other languages, VB lets you declare the type of variable associated with each variable name in one of two ways. First, you can explicitly define the variable types using Dim statements. Second, you can append a special character to the end of each variable name to declare its type. Table 7-1 lists the types of variables that are available in Visual Basic, and shows how they relate to FORTRAN variables.

Declaring variables is now easy. To define an integer variable at the top of a subroutine, you could now use the following line of code:

```
Dim JulDate As Double
```

This declares the variable JulDate as an eight-byte floating-point number (like REAL*8). Here are other sample declarations that make use of the additional variable types. Notice that multiple declarations can be placed on a single line.

```
Dim Average as Single
Dim Year as Integer, Month as Integer
Dim AmountDue as Currency
```

If you need a quick variable in FORTRAN, you can, within limits, just use the variable name and go back to place the definition at the top of your program when you have finished. This can sometimes give unexpected results, however.

Visual Basic allows you to declare variables just by using them, as long as the last character of the variable name is one of the characters listed in Table 7-2.

TABLE 7-1 Visual Basic Variable Types and Their FORTRAN Equivalents

Visual Basic Type	FORTRAN Equivalent	Description
Integer	INTEGER*2	A two-byte integer.
Long	INTEGER*4	A four-byte integer.
Single	REAL*4	A four-byte floating point.
Double	REAL*8	An eight-byte floating point.
Currency	No equivalent	A number with a fixed decimal point; used for monetary calculations.
String	CHARACTER*(*)	A character string.

TABLE 7-2 Characters Used for Declaring VB Variable Types

Character	VB Variable Type	FORTRAN Equivalent
%	Integer	INTEGER*2
&	Long	INTEGER*4
!	Single	REAL*4
#	Double	REAL*8
@	Currency	No equivalent
$	String	CHARACTER*(*)

This method of declaring variables allows you to use statements like the following,

```
Name$ = "FORTRAN for Windows"
Age% = 33
```

without having to pre-declare the Name$ and Age% variables.

 Note These characters are used not only to designate the type, but also to name the variables. This means that the character must always be part of the variable name when it is used.

An equivalent declaration would have been

```
Dim Name As String, Age As Integer
Name = "FORTRAN for Windows"
Age = 33
```

In this case, however, the final character would not have to be carried everywhere the variable name appears.

Writing the FORTRAN DLL Interface for VB

In order to call external, DLL-based functions and subroutines from other sources, Visual Basic requires that you declare an interface for the function in the GLOBAL.BAS area of your VB application. The GLOBAL area of your application is similar to a COMMON area in FORTRAN. It is here that all globally accessible variables are defined. In addition, all interfaces to external code are defined here.

Using the knowledge you have regarding the variable types available, you can write the following interfaces for the Julian date functions used throughout this book. (These declarations must each be written on a single line in your programs. They are split here due to publishing restrictions.)

```
Declare Sub CalendarDate Lib "Julian.DLL" (JulDate#, aYear%,
     aMonth%, aDay% )
Declare Function Julian Lib "Julian.DLL" (aYear%, aMonth%,
     aDay% ) as Double
```

These declarations are typed directly into the GLOBAL.BAS file, by first selecting it from the VB Project window (usually situated along the right side of the screen). Just double-click your mouse on the line that reads GLOBAL.BAS, and you will be presented with a form that accepts these global entries, as shown here:

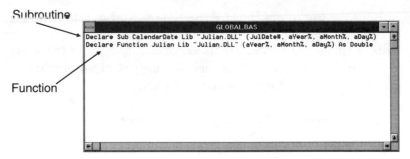

Subroutine

```
                                    GLOBAL.BAS
Declare Sub CalendarDate Lib "Julian.DLL" (JulDate#, aYear%, aMonth%, aDay%)
Declare Function Julian Lib "Julian.DLL" (aYear%, aMonth%, aDay%) As Double
```

Function

In each case, you must declare the external interface exactly. A Sub declaration denotes a subroutine, similar to a subroutine in FORTRAN. A Function declaration is like a FORTRAN function—a value is returned at the end of the function.

The Lib command gives the name of the DLL (or library file) that will be accessed for the function.

At the end of a function declaration is a note regarding the type of return value. In this case, with the JULIAN() function, you would return a Single (REAL*4) or a Double (REAL*8), depending on how you have built the DLL.

 Caution   Always use return values for your functions that match what is provided by your FORTRAN code. In this case, the Julian DLL was built with REAL*4 variables in Chapter 5, but will be rebuilt with REAL*8 variables in Chapter 8. You can use either version; just be sure to match your application interface with the correct version of your libraries. Incorrect matching of application calls and libraries can cause your entire system to stop running!

The parameters are provided within the parentheses for each of these calls. There are two ways to display the parameters and their types, as with the declaration of any variables—with special characters, or verbally. Therefore, the following declarations are equivalent:

```
' Version using special characters
Declare Function WeekDayNo ( JulDate# ) As Integer

' Version with explicit declaration
Declare Function WeekDayNo ( JulDate As Double ) As Integer
```

You should also remember that the default in Visual Basic, as in FORTRAN, is to pass all parameters by reference. If you want to pass a parameter by value, use the ByVal keyword in your declaration, like this:

```
Declare Function WeekDayNo ( ByVal JulDate# ) As Integer
```

Note   If you pass a string as ByVal, Visual Basic converts the string into C language format! This might be useful for you as you start mixing these languages.

Building a Complete Application

To show you the simplicity with which a VB application can be built to utilize your FORTRAN code, a complete program will be built around the Julian date DLL provided in Chapter 5. When running, the program will look like Figure 7-3.

The About menu item shows a form that displays information about the application. The code attached to the About menu choice is as simple as this:

```
Sub mnuAbout_Click ()
    Form2.Show
End Sub
```

where Form2 is the name of the form that will display the About information.

Note   Most Windows applications provide an About box. These windows are used to display copyright information, version numbers, author information, or whatever the application designer deems important. In this case, the About box (or form), which is shown in Figure 7-4, shows just the name of the application, a comment, and the author's name.

The main screen of the Julian application

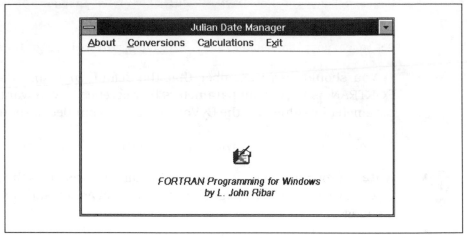

The Conversions menu option will utilize the Julian() and CalendarDate() functions to convert Julian dates to and from standard calendar dates. The Calculations menu option will allow the user to determine the number of days between two dates or add days to one date to calculate a second date.

The entire menu structure is designed using the VB Menu Design window (shown in Figure 7-5), which appears when the VB Window menu

The Julian Date Manager About box

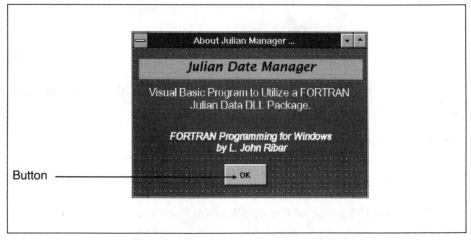

option is selected. The Menu Design window is all that is necessary for adding a complete menu to the main form.

Notice that each menu item has a CtlName, or control name, given to it. This name is used to generate the subroutines that you will use for different user actions. For instance, in the menu example for the About box, the only part of the code that had to be written was this line:

```
Form2.Show
```

The VB designer supplied this outline

```
Sub mnuAbout_Click ()

End Sub
```

based on the fact that the menu item's CtlName was mnuAbout, and that the code would respond to a mouse click on that menu item.

Once the menu is designed, clicking the mouse on one of the menu items brings up a box that allows you to add the code. This code controls the action that should occur when the menu item is selected by the user. As noted with the About box, much of the menu-handling code is used

FIGURE 7-5　The Visual Basic Menu Design window

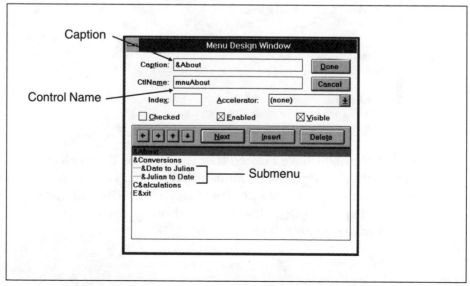

just to call up the other forms, and the name of the subroutine is already displayed by the designer.

Next, the forms for the conversion routines will be developed. The form for Calendar-to-Julian date conversion is shown in Figure 7-6. In this case, the only code written for the entire conversion is attached to the Convert button. The user just fills in the required date information and then presses the Convert button. The code will respond by updating the Julian Equivalent.

The Cancel button utilizes only a single line of code within its click subroutine, as shown here:

```
Sub Command2_Click()
   Form3.Hide
End Sub
```

It is actually Form3 that is being developed. The Hide command therefore hides the form from view. This, in effect, puts the user back at the main menu. Before leaving this form, however, you should see the VB code attached to the Convert button, shown here:

```
Sub Command1_Click()
   ' Comments start with a single quote character.
   ' First, convert the input fields into numbers.
   yy% = Val(YearIn.Text)
   mm% = Val(MonthIn.Text)
   dd% = Val(DayIn.Text)

   ' Now, call the Julian() function, as described
   ' in Global.BAS
   JulDate# = Julian( yy%, mm%, dd% )

   ' Finally, move the answer to the output field
   JulianOut.Caption = Str$( JulDate# )
End Sub
```

You might have noticed that the buttons themselves are called Command1 (Convert) and Command2 (Cancel). The input fields on the form are named YearIn, MonthIn, and DayIn, and the Julian date output object is called JulianOut. The Text attribute of each input field contains the information entered by the user.

Val() is used to convert the text into numbers that can be used for calculations. Because of the definition provided earlier, a call to Julian is very simple. Then the Caption attribute of JulianOut is assigned the string version of the final calculated Julian date. This process sounds much more complicated than it is; you might want to spend a few minutes looking at the preceding code, and at Figure 7-6, to solidify in your mind how this works.

The final form used for this application is shown in Figure 7-7.

In this form, two buttons are provided to allow for different types of calculations. The first button (Days Difference) waits for the First Date and Second Date fields to be filled and then places the number of days between the two dates in the Days In-Between field. The code for this function, which is attached directly to the Days Difference button, is shown here:

```
Sub Command1_Click ()
    ' Read the first date from the user
    m1% = Val(Month1.Text)
    d1% = Val(Day1.Text)
    y1% = Val(Year1.Text)

    ' Calculate first Julian
    J1# = Julian( y1%, m1%, d1% )
```

 FIGURE 7-6 Calendar-to-Julian-date conversion form

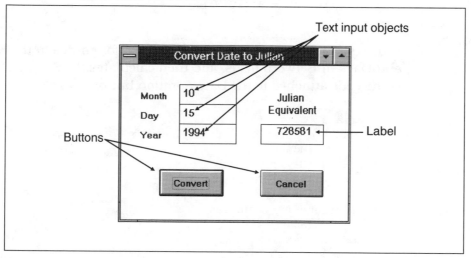

FIGURE
7-7
The final form

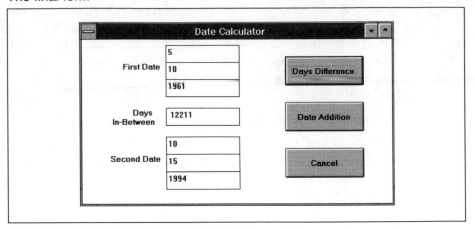

```
         ' Read the second date from the user
         m2% = Val(Month2.Text)
         d2% = Val(Day2.Text)
         y2% = Val(Year2.Text)

         ' Calculate second Julian
         J2# = Julian( y2%, m2%, d2% )

         ' Calculate and display the result
         DaysDiff.Text = Str$( J2# - J1# )
End Sub
```

The second button (Date Addition) waits for entries in the First Date and Days In-Between fields, and then calculates the Second Date. Here is the code attached to the Date Addition button:

```
Sub Command2_Click ()
         ' Read the first date from the user
         m1% = Val(Month1.Text)
         d1% = Val(Day1.Text)
         y1% = Val(Year1.Text)

         ' Calculate first Julian
         J1# = Julian( y1%, m1%, d1% )
         ' Add the required days
```

```
    J2# = J1# + Val( DaysDiff.Text)

    ' Now, calculate the second date
    Call CalendarDate( J2#, y2%, m2%, d2% )

    ' Finally, output the results
    Month2.Text = Str$(m2%)
    Day2.Text = Str$(d2%)
    Year2.Text = Str$(y2%)

End Sub
```

You have just developed a complete Julian-date-calculation application for Windows with minimal effort. In the process, you reused existing FORTRAN code, and generated a somewhat fancy user interface.

With a little practice, you can design quite elaborate applications with Visual Basic. You can dress up otherwise drab, text-mode programs by adding colors, pictures, and your own flair, with little additional training or effort. One nice feature of VB is that a very complete reference and design guide is presented online by the Windows Help facility. This allows you to work without the manual most of the time. For FORTRAN programmers, VB is especially ideal—you can design front ends for your libraries without having to learn a complete new language.

No More Languages

In the previous chapter, you saw how C can be combined with FORTRAN functions to create Windows applications. In this chapter, you saw how Visual Basic can be used to create streamlined front ends for your FORTRAN routines. By now, you might feel that you do need to learn another language in order to utilize features of Windows with your FORTRAN programs. While both C (or C++) and Visual Basic are excellent choices, there are also non-language opportunities for creating Windows applications. In the next chapter, you'll learn about using Microsoft Excel, or another spreadsheet application, as a front end for your FORTRAN functions.

CHAPTER

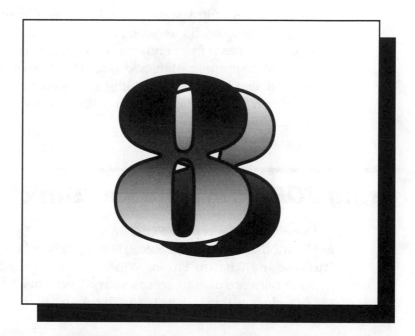

Using Microsoft Excel as a Front End for FORTRAN

T hus far, you have seen how to create Windows programs using not only your FORTRAN compiler, but also several other languages. In this chapter, you'll learn about using other applications to access your existing FORTRAN libraries.

Note The discussion in this chapter revolves around the Microsoft Excel application, a spreadsheet that is quite common under Windows. However, the topics and techniques you find here can also be used with many other Windows spreadsheet packages, including 1-2-3 for Windows and Quattro Pro for Windows.

There are several reasons to use Excel as a front end for FORTRAN. First, many people who use computers know how to use spreadsheets; by using Excel as a front end, you will reduce the training time needed by users of your applications. Second, Excel provides you with tools for building dialog boxes, thus adding a new dimension of user-interface construction to your application without getting into Windows API programming.

Using FORTRAN Routines Directly in Excel

Once you convert your FORTRAN code into Dynamic Link Libraries, applications like Microsoft Excel, Microsoft Word for Windows, Borland's Paradox and Quattro Pro for Windows, Lotus 1-2-3 for Windows, and many others are able to access your algorithms. In this chapter, you'll see exactly how this is done using Excel. Other applications you use may have similar abilities.

Spreadsheets

The newer spreadsheet programs, especially those running in Microsoft Windows, have moved far beyond simple numeric calculations, especially in two areas: presentation and programmability.

When an accountant filled rows and columns of a paper spreadsheet with numbers, titles could be added to help find where different pieces of data were placed. Fonts, text sizes, borders, and shading were limited to how adept the accountant was with a pencil. With the new electronic spreadsheets, changing any of these attributes (text size, font, colors, border lines, shading, and so on) is as easy as a mouse click.

A problem with paper spreadsheets is that there was no audit trail for how a specific number was generated. Now, you specify an algorithm for a calculation, and not only can it be read at any time, it can be changed, copied, moved to other locations, or completely removed.

The new spreadsheets, like Excel, provide not only calculation facilities, but the capability of adding actual programming functions to the spreadsheet. Generally, these programs, written within the actual spreadsheets themselves, are referred to as macros. Later in this chapter, you'll see exactly how a macro is written, and what the macro programming "language" looks like. But first, you should learn how to call a DLL function from within a spreadsheet formula.

Using DLL Calls in Formulas

A *formula* is a calculation embedded within a spreadsheet. Each position in a spreadsheet is called a *cell*. Each row is numbered (1, 2, 3, and so on), and each column is identified by a letter or series of letters (A, B, C, AA, AB, AC, etc.). Each specific cell therefore has a name, formed by combining the row and column names. For instance, the top-left corner of a spreadsheet (first column, first row) is called A1 (column A, row 1).

Each cell of a spreadsheet can hold one of the following:

☐ *Text* A series of letters, numbers, or other characters. (Numbers used as text in a spreadsheet cell are generally preceded by a special character, such as ', which instructs the software to disregard their numeric value.)

☐ *A number* Can be positive or negative, an integer or a floating-point number.

☐ *A formula* Directions on how to create a value within the cell.

Text and numbers are rather straightforward; formulas can be very simple or very complex. Figure 8-1 shows examples of these different

An Excel spreadsheet that uses DLL functions

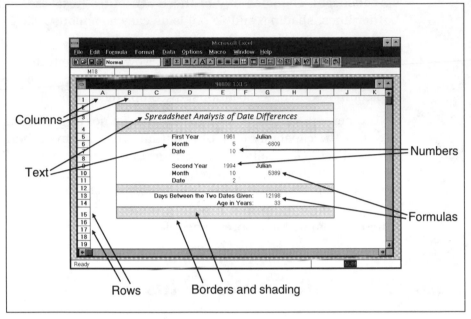

types of cells. Cells G6, G10, G13, and G14 contain the following formulas:

```
Cell G6:    =CALL("JULIAN.DLL","JULIAN","BMMM",E5,E6,E7)
Cell G10:   =CALL("JULIAN.DLL","JULIAN","BMMM",E9,E10,E11)
Cell G13:   =G10-G6
Cell G14:   =INT(G13/365.24)
```

The formulas in cells G13 and G14 are fairly simple (even though the cells they operate on are not). Each formula begins with the equal sign. In G13, the number displayed will be the result of subtracting the value in cell G6 from the value in cell G10. This type of formula works on the values referenced by the cell names given. Any time the numbers in cells G6 and G10 change, the formula in G13 will be reevaluated, and a new value will be displayed.

The formula in cell G14 takes the answer from cell G13 and divides it by the number of days in a year (365.24). The answer is forced into an integer result using the INT() function. Excel, like most spreadsheet applications, has a large number of built-in functions that are available. For a complete list, you should review the Microsoft Excel function reference manual.

The important function you need for dealing with DLL code, however, is the CALL() function. The CALL() function takes at least three parameters and returns a value that is displayed in the cell where the CALL() function is actually executed.

The first parameter is the name of the DLL to be called. If you recall, in Chapter 5 you built a Julian date DLL. That DLL will be used in the examples throughout this chapter. First, a change to the code is in order.

Excel uses eight-byte floating-point numbers. Therefore, you first need to modify the Julian source code, as shown here:

```
C-------------------------------------------------------------C
!      Julian.FOR
!
!      Julian Date Calculation Routines Library
!
!      Author:      L. John Ribar
!      System:      Microsoft FORTRAN 5.1
!      Date:        15 October 1994
!      OS:          DOS or Windows
!
!      These routines are based on a personal interpretation
!      of how Julian dates should work. While the "real"
!      Julian dates are not calculated exactly the same way,
!      the numbers generated here can be used for the same
!      purposes in most cases.
!
!      Modified to use eight-byte floating-point numbers.
!
C-------------------------------------------------------------C


!
!      Julian() returns the Julian date for a given date.
!

       REAL*8 FUNCTION Julian( Year, Month, Day )
       INTEGER*2 Year, Month, Day

       REAL*8    TotalDate
       INTEGER*2 DayOfYear        ! Function return type
```

```
!       First, determine days through the beginning of the
!       year. Years have about 365.2425 days each.
        TotalDate = Year * 365.2425

!       Now, add the days that have occurred in this year.
        TotalDate = TotalDate + DayOfYear( Year, Month, Day )

!       Finally, return the answer
        Julian = AINT(TotalDate)

        END                             ! FUNCTION Julian

C------------------------------------------------------------C


!
!       CalendarDate() takes a given Julian date and returns
!       the actual calendar date, meaning month, day, and
!       year.
!
        SUBROUTINE CalendarDate( JulDate, Year, Month, Day )
        REAL*8    JulDate
        INTEGER*2 Year, Month, Day

        REAL*8    LeftOver
        INTEGER*2 LOver

!       Since years have about 365.2425 days each, determine
!       the years that are in this Julian number.
        Year = AINT( JulDate / 365.2425 )

!       To determine the month and day, subtract the year,
!       and call the MonthAndDay() subroutine.
        LeftOver = JulDate - AINT(365.2425 * Year)
        LOver = AINT(LeftOver)
        CALL MonthAndDay( LOver, Year, Month, Day )

!       That's All!
        END                             ! SUBROUTINE Calendar Date

C------------------------------------------------------------C


!
!       WeekDayNo() returns the weekday of the Julian date
!       passed as a parameter. The first day of the week is
!       Sunday, which returns a 1. Thus, Saturday returns 7.
!
```

```
      INTEGER*2 FUNCTION WeekDayNo( JulDate )
      REAL*8    JulDate

      REAL*8    Temp

!     First, get the offset of the date, 0 = Friday
      Temp = MOD( JulDate, 7 )

!     Now adjust for actual weekdays
      Temp = Temp - 1
      IF (Temp.LE.0) Temp = Temp + 7
      WeekDayNo = Temp

      END                       ! FUNCTION WeekDayNo


C------------------------------------------------------------C


!
!     The DayOfYear() function returns the day of the year
!     that corresponds to the month and day passed into
!     the routine.
!
      INTEGER*2 FUNCTION DayOfYear( Year, Month, Day )
      INTEGER*2 Year, Month, Day

      LOGICAL*2 IsLeap          ! Function return value
      LOGICAL*2 LeapYear
      INTEGER*2 I, J            ! Count/Sum variables
      INTEGER*2 Days(12)        ! Monthly offsets

!     This array holds the number of days of the previous
!     month, used to determine the days that have passed
!     in the year in question.
      DATA Days / 0, 31, 28, 31, 30, 31,
     +            30, 31, 31, 30, 31, 30 /

!     Adjust for leap years
      LeapYear = IsLeap(Year)
      IF (LeapYear) THEN
          Days(3) = 29
      END IF

!     Now add up the days that have passed
      J = Day                   ! Start with Day of Month
      DO I=1,Month              ! Add for each month
```

```
            J = J + Days(I)
      END DO

      DayOfYear = J

      END                         ! FUNCTION DayOfYear()

C------------------------------------------------------------C

!
!     The IsLeap() function returns TRUE if the year in
!     question is a leap year, and FALSE otherwise.
!
      LOGICAL*2 FUNCTION IsLeap( Year )
      INTEGER*2 Year

      INTEGER*2 By4, By100, By400

      By4   = MOD(Year,4)
      By100 = MOD(Year,100)
      By400 = MOD(Year,400)

      IF ( ((By4.EQ.0).AND.(By100.NE.0)) .OR.
     +     (By400.EQ.0)) THEN
         IsLeap = .TRUE.
      ELSE
         IsLeap = .FALSE.
      END IF

      END                         ! FUNCTION ByLeap()

C------------------------------------------------------------C

!
!     MonthAndDay() determines the month and day of a
!     given annual day number.
!
      SUBROUTINE MonthAndDay( DayNum, Year, Month, Day )
      INTEGER*2 DayNum, Year, Month, Day

      INTEGER*2 Days(12)          ! Monthly offsets
      INTEGER*2 DN                ! Calculatron
      LOGICAL*2 IsLeap            ! Function return type
      LOGICAL*2 LeapYear
```

```
!       This array holds the number of days of each month,
!       used to determine the days that will pass in each.
        DATA Days / 31, 28, 31, 30, 31, 30,
     +               31, 31, 30, 31, 30, 31 /

!       Adjust for leap years
        LeapYear = IsLeap(Year)
        IF (LeapYear) THEN
            Days(2) = 29
        END IF

!       Now count down the days for each month
        DN = DayNum
        Month = 1

        DO WHILE (DN .GT. Days(Month)) ! Still not right month
            DN = DN - Days(Month)
            Month = Month + 1
        END DO
        Day = DN

        END                             ! SUBROUTINE MonthAndDay


C------------------------------------------------------------C
```

Build this DLL as you learned in Chapter 5, and be sure to copy it to your Windows directory; in this way, all your applications (including Excel) will have access to it.

The second parameter to the CALL() function is the name of the function that you want to call within the DLL. In this case, the function Julian() is called to calculate a Julian date, given a calendar date.

The third parameter is a series of characters representing the parameter types that will be used in the DLL call. The first character represents the return value, and the additional characters represent the types of data to be passed into the DLL function. In this case, there will be a floating-point return value (designated by a B in the first position of the third parameter), and three integer parameters passed into the function (designated by the three Ms).

The rest of the parameters passed to the CALL() function are the values that need to be passed to the actual DLL function, in this case, the year, month, and day to be converted into a Julian date.

It is important to note here that FORTRAN expects parameters to be passed by reference, not by value. This means that the address of the parameter is actually passed, as opposed to just a copy of the data value. In looking at the following table, you will notice parameters of both reference and value types. Generally, you will stick with reference values for your FORTRAN DLLs.

Table 8-1 shows the types of parameters that can be used in calling FORTRAN DLL functions, as they should be designated in the third parameter passed to CALL(). Look carefully at this list to determine the correct parameters; the wrong choices will often cause Excel to terminate unexpectedly. The important thing to notice is whether to use a reference parameter or a value parameter. As a general rule, use references for your function's parameters, and values for your function's return value.

TABLE 8-1 Parameters Used for Calling FORTRAN DLL Functions

Code	FORTRAN Type	Description
A	LOGICAL	Boolean data, passed by value. 1=TRUE, 0=FALSE. (Use for return values.)
B	REAL*8	8-byte floating-point, passed by value. (Use for return values.)
C	C String	Null-terminated string, passed by reference. Requires the C designator on FORTRAN strings.
E	REAL*8	8-byte floating-point, passed by reference. (Use for parameters.)
F	C String	Null-terminated string that can be modified in place, so that the text within Excel can be modified by your function.
I	INTEGER*2	2-byte integer, passed by value. (Use for return values.)
J	INTEGER*4	4-byte integer, passed by value. (Use for return values.)
L	LOGICAL	Boolean data, passed by reference. (Use for parameters.)
M	INTEGER*2	2-byte integer, passed by reference. (Use for parameters.)
N	INTEGER*4	4-byte integer, passed by reference. (Use for parameters.)

In this call to the CALL() function, the JULIAN DLL will be called, and the Julian function within that DLL will be used:

```
=CALL("JULIAN.DLL","JULIAN","BMMM",1994,10,5)
```

A floating-point return value is expected, and three integer parameters (1994, 10, and 5) will be passed to the function.

This is all that is required for using your DLL functions from within a Microsoft Excel spreadsheet. However, you can go much further toward making Excel a front end for your functions, and you will begin to do so in the next section.

Writing a Front End in Excel

Spreadsheets are wonderful things for saving time in making calculations. However, they offer you complete freedom, meaning that you also have the power to destroy all your hard work just by putting data in the wrong location or overwriting something you spent hours perfecting.

If you want to use Excel as a serious front end to your FORTRAN functions, you should learn about using dialog boxes and macros, which are covered next, to automate and simplify the user interface. After that discussion, dialog boxes and macros will be used to integrate a FORTRAN program into the Windows environment.

Dialog Boxes

Dialog boxes are the standard method by which a Windows application asks you, the user, for information. A dialog box is a small window, with a standard look, displayed on the screen. A dialog box will usually have a caption at the top, some text describing the information required from the user, places to enter the information, and some buttons. One button seen on most dialog boxes is the OK button, which is used to tell the application that you are finished entering information, or that you have read the text and are ready to continue. A Cancel button is used to let the application know that you do not wish to continue.

Excel comes with a Dialog Editor, ready for your use in the creation of custom Excel-based applications. A dialog box being developed in the editor might look like the one in Figure 8-2. This is the dialog box that will be used in the application created later in this chapter.

The Item menu (ALT-I) is used to add items to your dialog box. This can include text, buttons, entry fields, groups of fields, list boxes, and icons (small graphical drawings, used for effect). In the dialog box shown in Figure 8-2, you'll notice that each entry field is shown with its type. In this case, all the entry fields are of the Edit Integer type.

Once you have developed the dialog box to a point where it is ready to use, you need to use the Edit menu (ALT-E) with the Select Dialog choice, followed by the Edit and Copy options. This is the method by which you will move the dialog box into your Excel spreadsheet.

Now, return to your spreadsheet. Move into the cell where you wish to put the dialog information. Make sure there is enough space; you will

FIGURE
8-2

A simple dialog box in the Excel Dialog Editor

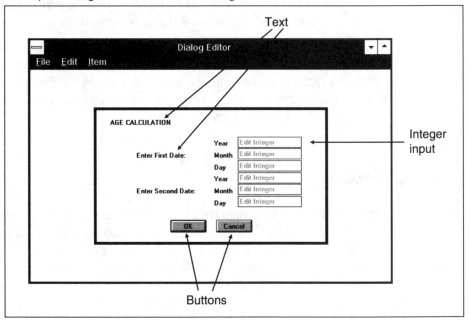

need seven columns, and as many lines as there are items in your dialog box (plus a few extra). Then, select Edit (ALT-E) and Paste to put the dialog information in the spreadsheet. The beautiful dialog box you drew will now look like Figure 8-3, a series of textual information, buttons, labels, title, and all!

The first five of the seven columns are used to show the item type, X and Y locations, and width and height of each item. Some of this information is not required, and shows up blank in the spreadsheet. The next column is text information, used in text fields. The seventh column is used by Excel to store data for field entries. This is where you can put default values, too.

Some possible item types (which are displayed in the first column of the spreadsheet) are listed in Table 8-2.

A dialog box rendered as Excel text

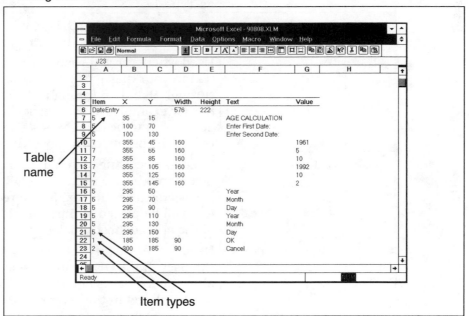

TABLE
8-2
Some of the Items Available for Excel Dialog Boxes

Type	Item	Purpose
1	OK button	Used when OK (not Cancel) is the default button. (The default button is selected when the user presses ENTER, unless the other button is actually selected.) Closes the dialog box, transfers the data from the edit fields to the seventh column, and allows the macro to continue. (See row 22 in Figure 8-3 for an example OK button.)
2	Cancel button	Used when OK is the default button. Allows the macro to continue processing, but does not transfer any data to the spreadsheet. (See row 23 in Figure 8-3 for an example.)
3	OK button	Used when Cancel (not OK) is the default button. Otherwise, functions the same as Type 1.
4	Cancel button	Used when Cancel is the default button. Otherwise, functions the same as Type 2.
5	Text	Used whenever you wish to place fixed text in your dialog box. (See rows 7 through 9 and 16 through 21 in Figure 8-3 for examples of text entries.) The actual text to be displayed is shown in the sixth column of the spreadsheet.
6	Text edit box	Used for receiving textual information to be entered by the user. If the OK button is selected after the text is entered, the text will be placed in the seventh column of the spreadsheet's dialog area.
7	Integer edit box	Used for the entry of integer numbers by the user. If the OK button is selected after the integer is entered, the integer will be placed in the seventh column of the spreadsheet's dialog area. (See rows 10 through 15 in Figure 8-3 for examples of integer entries.)

TABLE 8-2   Some of the Items Available for Excel Dialog Boxes (*continued*)

Type	Item	Purpose
8	Number edit box	Used for the entry of any numeric data by the user. If the OK button is selected after the number is entered, the number will be placed in the seventh column of the spreadsheet's spreadsheet area.
9	Formula edit box	Used for the entry of formulas by the user. If the OK button is selected after the formula is entered, the formula will be placed in the seventh column of the spreadsheet's dialog area.

There are other types of items available in Excel dialog boxes, but their use is beyond the scope of this book. For more information on these other types, which include list boxes, icons, and Help buttons, refer to the *Microsoft Excel User's Guide 2*.

Now that you have created a dialog box and have moved it into your spreadsheet, you need to learn about macros, which are the programs in Excel that will allow you to use the actual dialog boxes.

Macros

Macros are created with the programming languages provided with applications like Excel. Generally, a macro is a stored series of events that you want performed on a regular basis. A macro can be as simple as a memorized list of keystrokes used to perform a function, or can be as elaborate as any major software project.

Macros in Excel can be recorded by using the macro recorder function, which you access by selecting the Record option from the Macro menu (ALT-M, C). This option is used to capture a series of keystrokes or mouse selections that you want to repeat. Once you have recorded your macro, you can assign it to a specific keystroke. This means that you can play the entire sequence of events back with a single keystroke!

Another way of creating a macro is to enter it into the spreadsheet as text entries in a column of cells. Figure 8-4 shows a macro listing that will be used in the following discussion and in the next part of this chapter.

Notice that each macro command begins with the equal sign (=). Every macro starts at the top statement—in this case, the statement =DIALOG.BOX(DateEntry)—and continues downward through the cells until it encounters a return call, =RETURN( ).

You should also notice that there are names listed to the left of several of the macro lines (Dialog1, Julian1, Julian2, etc.). These names are listed only for documentation purposes. The actual names are attached to specific macro command lines using the Formula | Define Name menu command (ALT-R, D). The Define Name command helps make your macros more readable. Lets see how this works.

In Figure 8-5, you'll see the Define Name dialog box, where you can define names for specific cells in your spreadsheet. Looking again at our macro in Figure 8-4, you'll see the name Julian1 in cell A39. This name was actually assigned to cell B39 with the Define Name command. As a

FIGURE
8-4

A macro listing in Excel

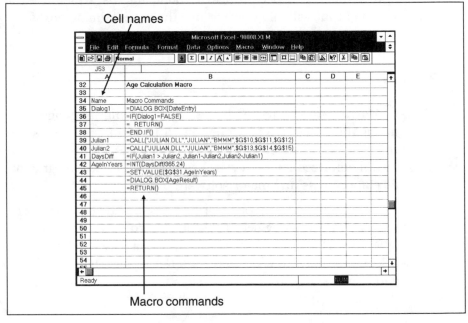

FIGURE
8-5

The Define Name dialog box

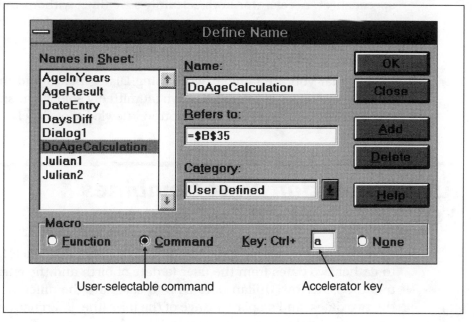

result, the name Julian1 can be used in any calculation without reference to the specific cell location (B39). Notice that the formula in cell B41 looks at the values Julian1 and Julian2, rather than using their cell names (B39 and B40). The names are listed to the left (in column A) only for documentation purposes.

The macro itself is named DoAgeCalculation. It was named using the Define Name dialog box shown in Figure 8-5. You'll notice that the name refers to cell B35, which is the first command in the macro.

At the bottom of the dialog box are two important things to note. First, the Command button has been selected (it shows as a darkened circle). This means that the macro will be placed in the menu of possible commands available when you select the Macro | Run menu command (ALT-M, R). The other names (Julian1, Julian2, and so on) do not have this button selected and therefore are not considered commands that can be executed.

The second thing to notice is that the box to the right of the *Key: CTRL+* heading contains the letter *a*. This means that the macro can be run by pressing the accelerator key CTRL-A from anywhere within the spreadsheet. Accelerator keys certainly save time; without this one, you would need to open the Macro menu, select Run, and then choose the name of the macro you wanted (in this case, DoAgeCalculation) from the resulting menu.

Now that you are familiar with using Dialog Boxes and macros, it's time to develop an entire application (admittedly somewhat small) using a FORTRAN DLL and your newly found knowledge of Excel.

An Application that Combines FORTRAN with Excel

In this section you will see the design of a simple application written to gather two dates from the user (a date of birth and the current date), use the FORTRAN Julian date DLL to calculate the difference between the two dates, and display the age of the user (the difference between the two dates, in years).

The dialog box for this application was developed in the first part of this chapter, and is shown in Figure 8-2. It asks the user for the year, month, and day for two dates. The number of years between these two dates will be calculated. The actual dialog box, when displayed by Excel, is shown in Figure 8-6. Notice that the dialog box now has a more three-dimensional appearance. This look is created totally by Excel; it requires no further programming or processing.

A second dialog box will also be developed. It will look like Figure 8-7, and will be used to display the final answer.

These dialog boxes are first drawn in Excel's Dialog Editor. Then, the following steps are executed for each dialog box to move it into an Excel spreadsheet:

1. Select Edit (ALT-E) from the Dialog Editor menu, and when the Edit menu appears, select Dialog. This selects the entire macro for moving to the spreadsheet.

2. Select Edit (ALT-E again), and then select Copy to move the dialog information to the Windows clipboard.

FIGURE
8-6

The date entry dialog box

AGE CALCULATION

Enter First Date:

Year	1961
Month	5
Day	10

Enter Second Date:

Year	1992
Month	10
Day	2

OK   Cancel

FIGURE
8-7

Displaying the final answer

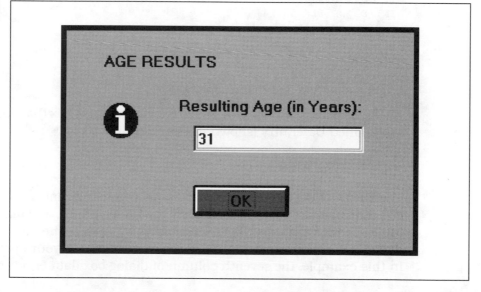

AGE RESULTS

Resulting Age (in Years):

31

OK

3. Open a spreadsheet in Excel.

4. Move to a location where the dialog information can be inserted into the spreadsheet.

5. From the main Excel menu, select Edit (ALT E) and then Paste to copy the dialog box information from the Windows clipboard into your spreadsheet.

6. Name the dialog box by selecting Formula (ALT-F), and then the Define Name option. In this example, name the first dialog box DateEntry and the second dialog AgeResult. Names are required so that you can access the dialog boxes from your macro program.

7. Repeat these steps for each dialog box required by your application, two in this case.

Now, a macro has to be written to take advantage of these dialogs and the Julian date library. The macro looks like this:

```
=DIALOG.BOX(DateEntry)
=IF(Dialog1=FALSE)
=  RETURN()
=END.IF()
=CALL("JULIAN.DLL","JULIAN","BMMM",$G$10,$G$11,$G$12)
=CALL("JULIAN.DLL","JULIAN","BMMM",$G$13,$G$14,$G$15)
=IF(Julian1>Julian2,Julian1-Julian2,Julian2-Julian1)
=INT(DaysDiff/365.24)
=SET.VALUE($G$31,AgeInYears)
=DIALOG.BOX(AgeResult)
=RETURN()
```

Let's examine this macro line by line.

The first line of the macro is used to call the dialog box that you created and named DateEntry (shown in Figure 8-6).

```
=DIALOG.BOX(DateEntry)
```

The DIALOG.BOX command is an Excel command that uses the seven columns of information generated by the Dialog Editor, and manages the interface with the user. If the OK button is pressed, the data from that dialog box will be moved into the seventh column of your spreadsheet. In this example, the seventh column of dialog box data is column G.

The DIALOG.BOX() function returns a value of TRUE if the OK button was selected, or FALSE if Cancel was selected or pressed.

The next three lines of the macro

```
=IF(Dialog1=FALSE)
=  RETURN()
=END.IF()
```

are used to check this outcome.

In order for this to work, though, the cell containing the first macro instruction (cell B35 in Figure 8-4) has to be named Dialog1. Then the three statements above can check the return value of DIALOG.BOX().

The RETURN() function simply returns control of the spreadsheet to the user. If the user presses the Cancel button, the user will receive control through this RETURN() function.

END.IF() is used to end IF() statement processing in a way that relates to the same statements (IF and END IF) in FORTRAN.

Assuming that the user has selected the OK button, the six numbers entered in the dialog box are now located in the dialog's seventh column of information. In this example, this is in column G, rows 10 through 15. Therefore, you can now call the Julian function for each of the dates, using these macro commands (the next two lines of the macro):

```
=CALL("JULIAN.DLL","JULIAN","BMMM",$G$10,$G$11,$G$12)
=CALL("JULIAN.DLL","JULIAN","BMMM",$G$13,$G$14,$G$15)
```

Remember that the parameters are integers, called by reference in a FORTRAN DLL, so parameter type M is used in these calls. The dollar signs in front of the column letter G and the row numbers are used to force Excel to use those locations specifically. If the dollar signs are not included, and you move your macro, you might be pointing to different locations, and the macro might not work correctly.

OK, you have now calculated the Julian dates for the dates supplied through your dialog box. Next, name these two cells (where the CALL( ) function is called) Julian1 and Julian2, so the Julian dates can be used in later calculations.

The next statement uses the Excel IF() function:

```
=IF(Julian1>Julian2,Julian1-Julian2,Julian2-Julian1)
```

IF() takes three parameters. The first one is a logical value, or comparison. The value of the cell becomes the second parameter if the logical comparison is true, or the third parameter if the comparison is false.

In this case, if the first date is later (and therefore larger) than the second date, the value will be found by subtracting the second date from the first date (Julian1–Julian2). Otherwise, assume that the first date came before the second, and the value for the cell will be the result of Julian2–Julian1. This calculation determines the number of days between these two dates.

Before continuing, name this cell as DaysDiff for use in the next calculation:

```
=INT(DaysDiff/365.24)
```

This command determines the number of years between the two dates, and then uses INT() to convert the difference to an integer for displaying to the user. Name this cell AgeInYears for use in the next statement. This command is used to move the information just calculated into the second dialog box:

```
=SET.VALUE($G$31,AgeInYears)
```

The SET.VALUE function copies the data in the AgeInYears cell to G31, which is the seventh column of data for the second dialog box, on the row of the integer edit field, where you will display the resulting age. Once this is done, you are finally ready to display the result, which will appear in the AgeResult dialog box. Use this command:

```
=DIALOG.BOX(AgeResult)
```

In this case, no Cancel button is available, so there is no need to check the return value of DIALOG.BOX. In fact, the only thing left to do, once the user selects the OK button, is to return to the spreadsheet with this statement:

```
=RETURN()
```

Remember Writing Excel applications to use with your FORTRAN functions might take a little time at first. One of the most important steps is to name all the cells that you will need to use later in the process. Specifically, these include the dialog boxes, the first cell in each macro you write, and any cells that will be used in calculations. After a little practice, you will be able to develop professional Windows-based front ends for your FORTRAN code with an ease not often found in other FORTRAN environments.

Downsizing

Throughout this book, you have been exposed to methods for utilizing your existing FORTRAN code in Windows. One good reason for making this change is to utilize the additional memory available in Windows. Another reason is to add a more consistent user interface to your applications, possibly by utilizing other applications (like Excel).

In the next chapter, you'll learn about downsizing (transporting) your FORTRAN mainframe and minicomputer programs to Microsoft Windows; you'll discover some of the tools that are available to help you, as well as some pitfalls to look out for as you begin the downsizing process.

Downsizing Mainframe Applications to the PC

Throughout this book, you have learned different ways to connect your FORTRAN functions to Windows programs. Perhaps the biggest question yet remaining is, why do so at all? In this chapter, you'll learn some of the benefits of moving your code to the personal computer platform. In addition, you'll find out about some tools that can help you with the migration process.

Deciding to Make a Change: Downsizing versus Right-Sizing

For several years, there has been much talk about *downsizing*, the process of moving mainframe applications down to minicomputers, or even down to microcomputers (better known as personal computers, or PCs).

Much of the rationale for this type of move has involved lowering the cost of hardware (the actual computer machinery). Thanks to recent changes to the Intel family of processors, upon which many personal computers (IBM family and compatibles) are based, there is now power within each PC to rival many minicomputers, as well as many older mainframes.

The availability of more powerful PCs has led to a trend of trying to move everything to the PC. Unfortunately, this type of blind jump has had a few drawbacks:

☐ Earlier versions of the popular FORTRAN compilers were not very compatible. This meant that a great deal of time had to be spent redesigning or rewriting the software to make use of the available compilers.

☐ Earlier microcomputers didn't have the horsepower to do some of the very intense calculations. This weakness was sometimes overcome by the addition of a math coprocessor to the PC. Unfortunately, this solution required the expense of the new hardware, and many programs had to be rewritten to make use of the new processor.

☐ Microcomputers were not inherently multiuser devices. This was mostly due to the single-user nature of the operating systems available. Multiuser versions were available, but only from lesser-known, often less supported vendors, which made their use somewhat risky.

As hardware has progressed, software has also moved forward. Therefore, in today's computing environment, you find the following solutions for the problems just mentioned:

☐   The newest FORTRAN compilers from Microsoft and WATCOM realize the popularity of downsizing, and have gone to great lengths to make their compilers work compatibly with their mainframe and minicomputer counterparts. In addition, Microsoft has added compatibility modes that force compatibility with VAX and IBM FORTRAN compilers, allowing mainframe development to take place on microcomputers.

☐   The newest processors from Intel have added built-in math coprocessor support. No additional hardware needs to be purchased. Along the same vein, the compilers have added full support for these processors, usually as a simple compilation flag.

☐   Better, more robust, well-supported, multiuser environments have begun to appear on PCs. The largest base of this type of software revolves around *network* operating systems. Networks allow each PC to remain single-user, while allowing programs and data to be shared with other users, utilizing special cables, interface cards, and network software. Some of the more popular networks include Novell Netware, Banyan Vines, IBM LAN Manager, and Microsoft's LAN Manager.

☐   Because the power of PCs has increased, the use of multitasking and multiuser operating systems has grown in popularity. These allow several programs, and even several users, to share the use of the processor in the PC. The operating systems that run most mainframe and minicomputers provide multitasking and multiuser capabilities, allowing many people to use the computer at the same time.

Some of the more popular multitasking operating systems, which allow several programs to run concurrently, but allow only one user, include IBM OS/2 and Microsoft Windows NT. The standard version of Microsoft Windows actually allows some multitasking, but it is driven more by the programmer than by the operating system itself.

The more popular multiuser platforms for the PC include Software Link PC-MOS and Digital Research MultiUser DOS, which are both PC-DOS based (meaning that they can run the tools described in this book), and several versions of UNIX (which do not use the tools described here, but might have similar tools available; FORTRAN has not been as widely available under UNIX, though).

Due to all of these advances, the idea of downsizing can now be more fully explored. However, you must realize that not all applications require downsizing or will even be helped by moving to a personal computer. For this reason, the task you have to perform should actually be called *right-sizing.*

Right-sizing your computing environment requires that you allow for different applications to remain at different levels. For instance, if you are running an application that is shared by all the users of a 200-user mainframe, there will be a great deal of expense involved in downsizing. This will include not only the cost of the FORTRAN conversions, but also the costs associated with redesigning the software to run on a PC network, with retraining all your users (who may be accustomed to using IBM or DEC terminals, for instance, but who now will have to learn something about PCs), and with upgrading the equipment for each user (to PCs with network interfaces, rather than dumb terminals).

On the other hand, if you have 200 users who are working with calculation programs but who don't necessarily use the same data (in an engineering environment, for instance), moving your FORTRAN routines to the PC could have major benefits.

Because of the great diversity possible in computerized work situations, you need to learn what the costs and benefits of downsizing might be so that you can make an informed decision about right-sizing. As a result, you might end up with more people working on PCs, some people still working on the mainframe, and some with access to both.

The Costs and Benefits of Downsizing

There are both good and bad sides to downsizing applications to the PC. As you go through this chapter, please keep the alternative of right-sizing in your mind. Weigh the costs and benefits, and then put your system together in the way that works best for your situation. No single reason is enough to downsize everything without a thorough investigation.

The Costs Involved in Downsizing

There are several costs that need to be justified as you consider downsizing. Some of these involve actual dollar expenses. Most costs, however, deal more with the programming and training time that will be required. Since you are familiar with your own unique staffing and equipment situation, you are the best judge for the actual costs that would be involved in downsizing.

Conversion of the FORTRAN Code

As mentioned earlier, there was a time not too long ago when the conversion of your existing FORTRAN source code might have been the most expensive item to swallow. With the advent of better compilers and other tools to "clean" your source code, this has changed.

While these improvements mean that the conversion should be cleaner, make sure you still plan for enough testing time. Your code might transfer to the PC, clean up nicely, and compile without errors, but still not work correctly! Remember that when you move from a mainframe or minicomputer, other factors might cause code problems.

Two major causes of problems are word size and word order.

If you consistently define all your variables using the INTEGER*2, INTEGER*4, REAL*4 parameters, and so on, rather than defaulting the definitions (using IMPLICITS, for instance), you should not have a problem with word sizing; otherwise, you need to be careful. Many mainframes and minicomputers use a word size of 16, 32, or even 66 bits, and if you have not been explicit in the declarations of your variables, this can cause problems. This does not mean that you *will* have problems, just that you need to plan some testing time to be sure nothing is amiss.

Word-order problems become a problem if you regularly share a memory location between two variable types. If your mainframe stores the low byte of an integer first in memory, followed by the high byte, using a PC that stores them in the opposite order could cause major problems. Again, such a difference may not cause any problems, but you need to make sure to test it thoroughly.

Adding Math and Network Support

The newer compilers allow transparent support of math coprocessors, usually with just a command-line switch. If you are not using one of these compilers, it will probably be worth the investment to upgrade, or trade in your PC FORTRAN compiler for one that does. This will save you a lot of time and effort in the long run!

Network support involves two different costs. First, if your application truly requires access by many people at the same time, you may need to add specific code to the application to handle such things as file sharing, record and file locking, etc. If you only wish to share applications and allow the users to have their own data, no additional programming should be required.

However, if the application is large and you do not want it installed on each PC, you will need to add network hardware. At a minimum, this will involve an additional network interface board for each PC. In addition, wiring will be required between the PCs. Also, depending on the network operating system you use, you may need to buy a dedicated file server (PC), that will house the hard disk drives for all your PCs; *dedicated,* in this case, means that the PC can only be used to service the network—no one will be able to use the server for running any applications directly.

Hardware and Software Costs

The one number you can generate simply is the cost of hardware and software required for downsizing. Software licenses for an operating system (PC-DOS, MS-DOS, OS/2, PC-MOS, or DRM-DOS), plus a license for Microsoft Windows, must be purchased for each user. More and more often, hardware vendors are bundling DOS and Windows with their computers, but be sure you have a license for each person.

The costs of hardware are coming down. For the cost of a standard IBM or DEC terminal, you can now buy a personal computer. In order to run Windows, though, you'll need a PC with more power; the minimum machine you should consider for use in a scientific environment (where much of FORTRAN lives) is an Intel 80486-based computer (not an 80486SX—this model includes no math chip). Your system should have at least 8 megabytes of memory, a 200-megabyte hard disk drive, a Super VGA monitor, and a mouse. This is not the minimum system required by Windows, but it should be the minimum considered for serious development work.

In addition, if you plan to share applications or data through a network, you will need to invest in network interface boards for each PC. Also, based on the network you choose, you will need wiring, usually coaxial or twisted pair (like phone cable), network operating system software, and possibly a dedicated file-server PC. This PC will have the minimum requirements listed above and will be used only by the network, not by any workers.

Training

Don't forget training! Not only will your users need to learn Windows, they will also need to learn some DOS. This cannot be underestimated. DOS and Windows can be fairly simple to use, at least at the level your users should need, but a structured teaching environment, with lots of hands-on training, is the preferred solution. Anything less allows minor mistakes to cause major problems.

The Benefits of Downsizing

After reading the previous section, you might be wondering why you wanted to downsize at all. Don't worry; there are many benefits, too! Use the costs paired against the benefits to determine where downsizing is preferred over not changing; in other words, use *right*-sizing!

The Windows Memory Manager

Until recently, many FORTRAN applications could not be taken to the PC simply because of memory constraints. Programs written on a VAX, using the virtual memory system provided there, have little worry about the amount of memory available.

On a PC however, there has been a limit of 640K of available memory. Microsoft Windows changes this. If you use the Microsoft or WATCOM compiler, all of the memory installed on the PC, plus a good deal of virtual memory from your hard disk, is available to your applications. Now, there are few applications that cannot be moved to the Windows environment due to memory constraints.

The benefit here is that a personal computer can now be used to perform calculations that previously required a minicomputer or mainframe. This is especially useful, considering the price of a PC versus the price of a larger computer.

Consistent User Interface

There is a growing desire in the industry to design software to work alike. One way to enforce this is through the use of a graphical user interface (GUI) such as Microsoft Windows.

Why is this similarity a benefit? The biggest reason is that it saves a lot of training dollars. Once a user can handle a given Windows application, he or she can generally utilize any Windows programs with minimal retraining.

This is, of course, possible under any programming environment, given a strong enough set of rules. An environment like Windows, however, allows all your applications to work the same way, including applications that you have no control of, such as file managers, word processors, and spreadsheets. What kind of work would it require under FORTRAN to create new front ends to all your applications so they would all work alike? Such uniformity is the benefit of using a GUI.

Multiple-Use Machines versus Single-Use Machines

Another significant benefit of downsizing is that PCs are more versatile than terminals attached to a host computer. Terminals served by a single, large computer can be used for several purposes—running FORTRAN applications, using mail programs, writing letters, and so on, but all the processing is done by the minicomputer or mainframe to which it is attached. If the main computer goes down, all the users are down, too. Also, the more people who use the computer, the slower the processing and response time becomes.

With PCs, you can perform all the same functions utilizing the local processor within the PC. If more people want to use PCs, there is no impact on you. If someone else's PC goes down, yours can continue to work; and, as mentioned earlier, providing PCs rather than terminals for users, which allows them additional functionality at the same time, is becoming very cost-effective.

Don't think that you will lose all those multiuser functions you've enjoyed. Today's PC networks allow file sharing, application sharing, network mail, security, and most other mainframe-style functions you are used to having.

In addition, terminal-emulation software is available, so your PC can *act* like a dumb terminal and still talk to your host computer, should the need arise. This arrangement might be useful for network mail, if your network extends beyond the local site, or for any job-tracking or work-tracking functions that are managed on the host.

Offloading of Computation and Display

It is important to note how great a difference the offloading of processing can provide. By allowing the PC to perform its own processing, you leave the host computer free to better (and more quickly) handle those functions it retains.

The most effective use of PCs is in areas where calculations can be best managed by math processors specially designed for numerical calculations. Also, many graphics-display algorithms require number crunching. By offloading this work to the PC, users who are used to viewing results in a test-based table can now enjoy the benefits of a graphical display with little or no additional hardware costs

If you really need speed, specially designed graphic coprocessor boards are also available for the PC, making Windows display graphics up to hundreds of times faster. These boards, along with the math coprocessors, make the PC a viable alternative to very expensive, dedicated workstations or color graphics terminals.

Tools to Help with Your Conversions

In this section, you will learn about some tools that are currently available to simplify your downsizing effort. These tools fall into two general categories: those that help clean up your existing FORTRAN code, and those that convert your FORTRAN code to C or C++.

 Note The tools discussed in this chapter are not the only tools available. Their appearance here is to show you the types of devices currently available, and does not constitute any recommendation as to their fitness for your applications. The address of each vendor is supplied—call them for the details in regard to your specific needs.

Updating the FORTRAN Code You Now Have

Very often, FORTRAN code ends up being very hard to read after years of use. Why? Often because the original designers have left, changes were needed along the way, not everything was documented, different development strategies and methodologies were used...and you end up with something commonly known as spaghetti code.

While a knowledgeable FORTRAN programmer can decipher this type of code, there will be a lot of time wasted determining what the original programmer, and the programmers that have come and gone since, were trying to do.

To avoid this sort of confusion, you might wish to look into one of the tools available for performing a cleanup effort on your code. Some of these tools include FORWARN and the FORTRAN Development Tools from Quibus, FOR_STRUCT from Cobalt Blue, and plusFORT from Polyhedron Software, Ltd.

FORWARN is an analysis tool that can help you find potential problems in your FORTRAN source code. Quibus quotes John Backus in their manual: "Unfortunately, we were hopelessly optimistic in 1954 about the problems of debugging FORTRAN programs..." This is probably one of the greatest understatements in programming history, not just about

FORTRAN, but about programming in general. FORWARN, and the other tools here, help find the problems before you start debugging, greatly saving time and effort. Some of FORWARN's features are detailed next.

FORWARN checks your FORTRAN applications for global and local problems. Global problems include incorrect types of parameters or a wrong number being sent into subroutines. In addition, the use of **COMMON** blocks is checked for consistency between modules. FORWARN also produces variable, subroutine, and function call cross-references, and a function call diagram, showing where functions and subroutines are called. The local checks look for variables that might be spelled incorrectly; since FORTRAN usually allows the use of variables without declaring them first, misspelling can be a major cause of software defects (bugs). Extensions to the FORTRAN-77 standard are also flagged; these are a major cause of portability problems.

The FORTRAN Development Tools package consists of several programs that aid in code cleanup. PRETTY is a tool that formats your FORTRAN code based on a style that you create. This allows the selection of indentation, statement renumbering, use of upper- and lowercase keywords and/or variable and subroutine names, and the conversion of nested **IF-THEN** statements to the more modern **IF-THEN-ELSE** statements. OUTLINE is a program that generates a listing of your program, drawing graphics lines to indicate the flow of **IF-THEN-ELSE** statements. It can also add line numbers and page breaks to create a useful documentation file for your code.

SPLIT breaks large FORTRAN into smaller pieces by generating a separate file for each function or subroutine in the original file. SEQ and UNSEQ are used to add and remove line numbers (sequence numbers in columns 73 through 80 of each line) from your code.

FOR_STRUCT is a tool for bringing your older FORTRAN code into the more modern, structured programming era. It does this by cleaning up your FORTRAN code, replacing older **DO-CONTINUE** blocks with **DO-ENDDO**, **DO-WHILE-ENDDO**, and **IF-THEN-ELSE** statements. Using these techniques, your code can end up with few statement labels, or none at all (other than those for FORMAT statements, for instance). FOR_STRUCT is very flexible in allowing you to generate FORTRAN fixes specific to several specific FORTRAN standards (such as FORTRAN-77,

MILSPEC FORTRAN, VAX FORTRAN, and FORTRAN-90). FOR_STRUCT is available on a number of hardware and software platforms, allowing you to clean up your code even if you aren't going to downsize it all. If you plan to convert your FORTRAN code to C or C++, it is recommended that you first use a tool like FOR_STRUCT or PRETTY to make the code simpler to convert.

plusFORT is a set of programs, like the FORTRAN Developer's Tools, that allow you multiple ways to update your code. SPAG, a program in this set, is used to help convert spaghetti code into more structured FORTRAN source. You can enable the use of FORTRAN-77, VAX FOR-TRAN, and FORTRAN-90 extensions during this restructuring. A typing facility makes sure that all variables have been declared, adding declarations where necessary. Unused code and variables are removed from the code. A beautifier helps make your code more self-documenting, and a static-analysis tool helps find the types of problems that can hurt during debugging.

Using one or more of the tools listed in this section will allow you to bring older FORTRAN code into the more modern, structured design era. This is a good path to follow for your maintenance programming, whether or not you plan to downsize your applications. Cleaning up your FOR-TRAN code first will create a better environment from which to work.

Converting to C or C++

It is also possible that you will want to move your application from FORTRAN to C or C++. This is not a minor undertaking! In fact, if you plan to make this move, consider it an upgrade to your software, not part of the downsizing effort.

C, at first glance, is a sensible choice for several reasons. First and foremost, C is probably one of the most portable languages currently supported. If you convert your application from FORTRAN to C, you will have a seemingly infinite number of hardware and software platforms that support the C code.

In addition, C is the original language of choice for Windows programming. Most of the example code you'll see in books and magazines will be shown in C.

In Chapter 6, you saw what C looks like. While it is not too difficult to read (if you are disciplined in your coding techniques), there are many types of operations that will look very different from their equivalents in FORTRAN. For this reason, if you really want to convert your FORTRAN code, you might consider C++ instead.

Why C++?

A simple explanation of C++ is that it is an upgrade of C. This means that most C code (in fact, all C code that conforms to the ANSI standard) can be compiled by a C++ compiler. C++ also adds object-oriented facilities to C.

This book is not the place to describe all the flexibility added with object orientation. But one major concept, polymorphism, should be mentioned.

In C, you cannot concatenate two strings with a plus sign, as you can do in FORTRAN. For this reason, some things that are done in FORTRAN will not be readily apparent in C. C++ allows polymorphism, which means that more than one function or operator can have the same name; the choice of which one to use is based on the types of parameters passed in at run time.

Polymorphism allows C++ programmers to actually rewrite how the plus sign works, to allow strings to be concatenated, for instance. This may seem like magic, or something too complicated to use in code conversion, and it might well be, but if you plan to port your code to another language, and your choices are C and C++, you will probably be better served with C++. This is especially true if you use an automated code converter, as discussed in the next section. FOR_C++, for instance, takes advantage of C++ facilities to make your conversion simpler, and the resulting code is more to a FORTRAN programmer's understanding.

Using an Automated Tool

Cobalt Blue produces two products, called FOR_C and FOR_C++, which help to automate the conversion process between FORTRAN and C or C++. To give you a feel for how this works, compare the next listing (the Julian date DLL code, in FORTRAN) to the code that follows it (a Cobalt Blue FOR_C translation).

```
C----------------------------------------------------------C
!        Julian.FOR
!
!        Julian Date Calculation Routines Library
!
!        Author:       L. John Ribar
!        System:       Microsoft FORTRAN 5.1
!        Date:         15 October 1994
!        OS:           DOS or Windows
!
!        These routines are based on a personal interpretation
!        of how Julian dates should work. While the "real"
!        Julian dates are not calculated, a reasonable use
!        of these numbers for the same purposes can be assumed.
!
C----------------------------------------------------------C


!
!        Julian() returns the Julian date for a given date.
!

         REAL*8 FUNCTION Julian( Year, Month, Day )
         INTEGER*2 Year, Month, Day

         REAL*8    TotalDate
         INTEGER*2 DayOfYear        ! Function return type

!        First, determine days through the beginning of the
!        year. Years have about 365.2425 days each.
         TotalDate = Year * 365.2425

!        Now, add the days that have occurred in this year.
         TotalDate = TotalDate + DayOfYear( Year, Month, Day )

!        Finally, return the answer
         Julian = AINT(TotalDate)

         END                        ! FUNCTION Julian

C----------------------------------------------------------C

!
!        CalendarDate() takes a given Julian date and returns
```

```
!     the actual calendar date, meaning month, day, and
!     year.
!
      SUBROUTINE CalendarDate( JulDate, Year, Month, Day )
      REAL*8    JulDate
      INTEGER*2 Year, Month, Day

      REAL*8    LeftOver
      INTEGER*2 LOver

!     Since years have about 365.2425 days each, determine
!     the years that are in this Julian number.
      Year = AINT( JulDate / 365.2425 )

!     To determine the month and day, subtract the year,
!     and call the MonthAndDay() subroutine.
      LeftOver = JulDate - AINT(365.2425 * Year)
      LOver = AINT(LeftOver)
      CALL MonthAndDay( LOver, Year, Month, Day )

!     That's All!
      END                         ! SUBROUTINE Calendar Date


C------------------------------------------------------------C


!
!     WeekDayNo() returns the weekday of the Julian date
!     passed as a parameter. The first day of the week is
!     Sunday, which returns a 1. Thus, Saturday returns 7.
!
      INTEGER*2 FUNCTION WeekDayNo( JulDate )
      REAL*8    JulDate

      REAL*8    Temp
      REAL*8    Seven

!     First, get the offset of the date, 0 = Friday
      Seven = 7.0
      Temp = MOD( JulDate, Seven )

!     Now adjust for actual weekdays
      Temp = Temp - 1
      IF (Temp.LE.0) Temp = Temp + 7
      WeekDayNo = Temp

      END                         ! FUNCTION WeekDayNo
```

```
C------------------------------------------------------------C

!
!       The DayOfYear() function returns the day of the year
!       that corresponds to the month and day passed into
!       the routine.
!
        INTEGER*2 FUNCTION DayOfYear( Year, Month, Day )
        INTEGER*2 Year, Month, Day

        LOGICAL*2 IsLeap          ! Function return value
        LOGICAL*2 LeapYear
        INTEGER*2 I, J            ! Count/Sum variables
        INTEGER*2 Days(12)        ! Monthly offsets

!       This array holds the number of days of the previous
!       month, used to determine the days that have passed
!       in the year in question.
        DATA Days / 0, 31, 28, 31, 30, 31,
       +            30, 31, 31, 30, 31, 30 /

!       Adjust for leap years
        LeapYear = IsLeap(Year)
        IF (LeapYear) THEN
           Days(3) = 29
        END IF

!       Now add up the days that have passed
        J = Day                   ! Start with Day of Month
        DO I=1,Month              ! Add for each month
           J = J + Days(I)
        END DO

        DayOfYear = J

        END                       ! FUNCTION DayOfYear()

C------------------------------------------------------------C

!
!       The IsLeap() function returns TRUE if the year in
!       question is a leap year, and FALSE otherwise.
!
        LOGICAL*2 FUNCTION IsLeap( Year )
        INTEGER*2 Year

        INTEGER*2 By4, By100, By400
```

```
        INTEGER*2 Four, Hundred, FourHund

        Four = 4
        Hundred = 100
        FourHund = 400

        By4   = MOD(Year,Four)
        By100 = MOD(Year,Hundred)
        By400 = MOD(Year,FourHund)

        IF ( ((By4.EQ.0).AND.(By100.NE.0)) .OR.
       +      (By400.EQ.0)) THEN
           IsLeap = .TRUE.
        ELSE
           IsLeap = .FALSE.
        END IF

        END                         ! FUNCTION ByLeap()


C------------------------------------------------------------C

     !
     !    MonthAndDay() determines the month and day of a
     !    given annual day number.
     !
        SUBROUTINE MonthAndDay( DayNum, Year, Month, Day )
        INTEGER*2 DayNum, Year, Month, Day

        INTEGER*2 Days(12)        ! Monthly offsets
        INTEGER*2 DN              ! Calculatron
        LOGICAL*2 IsLeap          ! Function return type
        LOGICAL*2 LeapYear

     !    This array holds the number of days of each month,
     !    used to determine the days that will pass in each.
        DATA Days / 31, 28, 31, 30, 31, 30,
       +            31, 31, 30, 31, 30, 31 /

     !    Adjust for leap years
        LeapYear = IsLeap(Year)
        IF (LeapYear) THEN
           Days(2) = 29
        END IF

     !    Now count down the days for each month
        DN = DayNum
        Month = 1
```

```
      DO WHILE (DN .GT. Days(Month)) ! Still not right month
         DN = DN - Days(Month)
         Month = Month + 1
      END DO
      Day = DN

      END                           ! SUBROUTINE MonthAndDay
```

```
C-----------------------------------------------------------C
```

Here is the Cobalt Blue FOR_C translation:

```
/*Translated by FOR_C, v3.4 (-), on 10/19/94 at 14:19:19 */
/*FOR_C Options SET: c=2 do=r ftn=ln op=iv s=dvz str=l */
#include <stdio.h>
#include <stdlib.h>
#include <math.h>
#include <fcrt.h>
/*---------------------------------------------------------C
 * Julian.FOR
 *
 * Julian Date Calculation Routines Library
 *
 * Author:    L. John Ribar
 * System:    Microsoft FORTRAN 5.1
 * Date:      15 October 1994
 * OS:        DOS or Windows
 *
 * These routines are based on a personal interpretation
 * of how Julian dates should work. While the "real"
 * Julian dates are not calculated, a reasonable use
 * of these numbers for the same purposes can be assumed.
 *
 *-------------------------------------------------------C */


/*     Julian() returns the Julian date for a given date.
 * */

double /*FUNCTION*/ julian(year, month, day)
short int *year, *month, *day;
{
  short int dayofyear(); /* Function return type */
  double julian_v, totaldate;

  /* First, determine days through the beginning of the
```

```
   * year. Years have about 365.2425 days each. */
  totaldate = *year*365.2425;

  /* Now, add the days that have occurred in this year. */
  totaldate = totaldate + dayofyear( year, month, day );

  /* Finally, return the answer */
  julian_v = trunc( totaldate );

  return( julian_v );
} /* end of function */, /* FUNCTION Julian */

/*-------------------------------------------------------C */


/*  CalendarDate() takes a given Julian date and returns
 *  the actual calendar date, meaning month, day, and
 *  year.
 * */
void /*FUNCTION*/ calendardate(juldate, year, month, day)
double *juldate;
short int *year, *month, *day;
{
  short int lover;
  double leftover;
  void monthandday();

  /*  Since years have about 365.2425 days each, determine
   *  the years that are in this Julian number. */
  *year = trunc( *juldate/365.2425 );

  /*  To determine the month and day, subtract the year,
   *  and call the MonthAndDay() subroutine. */
  leftover = *juldate - trunc( 365.2425**year );
  lover = trunc( leftover );
  monthandday( &lover, year, month, day );

  /*      That's All! */
  return;
} /* end of function */, /* SUBROUTINE Calendar Date */

/*-------------------------------------------------------C */


/* WeekDayNo() returns the weekday of the Julian date
 * passed as a parameter. The first day of the week is
 * Sunday, which returns a 1. Thus, Saturday returns 7.
```

```
 * */
short /*FUNCTION*/ weekdayno(juldate)
double *juldate;
{
  short int weekdayno_v;
  double seven, temp;

  /*  First, get the offset of the date, 0 = Friday */
  seven = 7.0;
  temp = fmod( *juldate, seven );

  /*  Now adjust for actual weekdays */
  temp = temp - 1L;
  if( temp <= 0L )
    temp = temp + 7L;
  weekdayno_v = temp;

  return( weekdayno_v );
} /* end of function */, /* FUNCTION WeekDayNo */

/*-----------------------------------------------------C */


/*  The DayOfYear() function returns the day of the year
 *  that corresponds to the month and day passed into
 *  the routine.
 * */
short /*FUNCTION*/ dayofyear(year, month, day)
short int *year, *month, *day;
{
  LOGICAL16 isleap(), /* Function return value */
   leapyear;
  short int dayofyear_v, i, i_, j; /* Count/Sum variables */
  static short days[12]={0,31,28,31,30,31,30,31,31,30,31,30};
    /* OFFSET Vectors w/subscript range: 1 to dimension */
  short *const Days = &days[0] - 1;
    /* end of OFFSET VECTORS */

  /*     This array holds the number of days of the previous
   *     month, used to determine the days that have passed
   *     in the year in question. */
  /*     Adjust for leap years */
  leapyear = isleap( year );
  if( leapyear ){
    Days[3L] = 29L;
    }
```

```
    /*      Now add up the days that have passed */
    j = *day;, /* Start with Day of Month */
    for( i = 1L; i <= *month; i++ ){
      i_ = i - 1;, /* Add for each month */
      j = j + Days[i];
      }

    dayofyear_v = j;

    return( dayofyear_v );
} /* end of function */, /* FUNCTION DayOfYear() */

/*------------------------------------------------------C */


/* The IsLeap() function returns TRUE if the year in
 * question is a leap year, and FALSE otherwise.
 * */
LOGICAL16 /*FUNCTION*/ isleap(year)
short int *year;
{
  LOGICAL16 isleap_v;
  short int by100, by4, by400, four, fourhund, hundred;

  four = 4L;
  hundred = 100L;
  fourhund = 400L;

  by4 = *year%four;
  by100 = *year%hundred;
  by400 = *year%fourhund;

  if( ((by4 == 0L) && (by100 !_ 0L)) || (by400 == 0L) ){
    isleap_v = TRUE;
    }
  else{
    isleap_v = FALSE;
    }

  return( isleap_v );
} /* end of function */, /* FUNCTION ByLeap() */

/*------------------------------------------------------C */


/*      MonthAndDay() determines the month and day of a
 *      given annual day number.
```

```
 *  */
void /*FUNCTION*/ monthandday(daynum, year, month, day)
short int *daynum, *year, *month, *day;
{
  LOGICAL16 isleap(), /* Function return type */
   leapyear;
  short int dn; /* Calculatron */
  static short days[12]={31,28,31,30,31,30,31,31,30,
                            31,30,31};
   /* OFFSET Vectors w/subscript range: 1 to dimension */
  short *const Days = &days[0] - 1;
   /* end of OFFSET VECTORS */

  /* This array holds the number of days of each month,
   * used to determine the days that will pass in each. */
  /* Adjust for leap years */
  leapyear = isleap( year );
  if( leapyear ){
    Days[2L] = 29L;
    }

  /* Now count down the days for each month */
  dn = *daynum;
  *month = 1L;

  while( dn > Days[*month] ){, /* Still not right month */
    dn = dn - Days[*month];
    *month = *month + 1L;
    }
  *day = dn;

  return;
} /* end of function */, /* SUBROUTINE MonthAndDay */

/*-------------------------------------------------------C */
```

As you can see, the FOR_C translation looks fairly clean. Remember, however, that this code was written to be clean and self-explanatory for you as a reader of this book. Your application code, or the code you have inherited, might not result in such a clean translation.

By the way, looking at the two examples above might give you more insight into the conversion process. This conversion was done automatically—do you understand what was changed and why? If so, you are well on the way to becoming a C programmer. If not, you might want to postpone your conversion to C, or find someone familiar with both languages (actually, *fluent* in both!) to help you with your conversion.

If this is the case, using one of the clean-up tools mentioned in the previous section should help to streamline the translation process.

 Remember As mentioned earlier in this chapter, it is very important to leave enough time in your agenda for testing. If you are converting your FORTRAN code to C or C++, be sure to have a C/C++ expert nearby to help with the final tweaking. This does not mean someone who has attended a three-day training session—spend the money to get a *real* expert, and the translation will go much more smoothly. You will be able to start using the code on your new platform much sooner, and with much greater reliability. Be sure to get someone fluent in both C and FORTRAN; otherwise, they might know only the half that you don't, and might not help you much at all!

Now It's Your Turn

Throughout this book, you have learned different ways to connect your FORTRAN functions to Windows programs. In this chapter, you have seen some of the benefits of moving your existing code to the Windows platform. In addition, you have seen some tools that might help in this migration.

Remember that the keyword is *right*-sizing, not just downsizing. Some applications will continue to work better on mainframes or minicomputers, or perhaps the justification for converting them is simply not as apparent as it might be. However, other tasks that have been put on larger computers only because those computers were available hold lots of promise for desktop replacement.

The move is now up to you.

Sources for the Products Mentioned

The following information is provided to help you in your search for the right tools to use in downsizing, or right-sizing, your applications. The appearance of specific vendors here (and the absence of others) does not constitute endorsement of these products. The purpose of this list is to give you a place to start in planning your conversion efforts.

Products	Vendors
Microsoft FORTRAN	Microsoft Corporation
Microsoft C/C++	One Microsoft Way
Microsoft Windows	Redmond, WA 98052
Microsoft Excel	(206) 882-8080
Visual Basic	
WATCOM FORTRAN	WATCOM Systems, Inc.
WATCOM C	415 Phillip Street
	Waterloo, Ontario
	CANADA
	(519) 886-3700
FORTRAN Tools	Quibus Enterprises, Inc.
FORWARN	3340 Marble Terrace
	Colorado Springs, CO 80906
	(719) 527-1384
FOR_STRUCT	Cobalt Blue, Inc.
FOR_C	875 Old Roswell Road
FOR_C++	Suite 400-D
	Roswell, GA 30076
	(404) 518-1116

Products	Vendors
plusFORT	Polyhedron Software Ltd.
	Linden House
	93 High Street
	Standlake, WITNEY, OX8 7RH
	United Kingdom
	(44) 0865-300579
DR MultiUser DOS	Digital Research
	70 Garden Court
	Monterey, CA 93942
	(408) 649-3896
PC-MOS	Software Link
	3577 Parkway Lane
	Norcross, GA 30092
	(404) 448-5465

Index

1-2-3 for Windows, 182
80486, 210
80486SX, 210

A

About box, 57, 59, 173
About option, 48
AboutBoxQQ, 57, 58, 63
Accelerator key, 197, 198
Accountant, 182
Alias, 134
ANSI standard, 217
API (Application Programming Interface), 3
APPEND, 35
Application name, 41
Application Programming Interface (API), 3
Application sharing, 212-213
Applications, 182
APPLOADER, 103
argc, 125
argv, 125

Arrange Icons option, 46
Array subscripts, 30
Attributes, 165
Audit trail, 183

B

BackColor, 166
Banyan Vines, 207
BASIC, 162
BAT Files
    BLDC, 138
    BLDFOR, 137
    CDLL, 139
    FORDLL, 138
Beautifier, 216
BLDC, 138, 142, 152, 155
BLDFOR, 137, 159
BLOCK DATA, 27, 35
BLOCKSIZE, 36
Borders, 182, 184
Braces, 128
Built-in function, 185
Button

Make the move to Windows™ and allow your DOS FORTRAN programs to break through the 640K barrier!

Now you can get a copy of Microsoft's latest professional FORTRAN compiler for Windows and DOS for just $249, a savings of over $200 off the suggested retail price!*

All you have to do is fill out this coupon and return it with your check or money order to the address on the rear. Or if you have a major credit card, just fill in the details, mail this card, and sit back and wait for your copy of Microsoft ® FORTRAN Professional Development System.

....

Please print

Name _____

Street Address _____

City/State/ZIP _____

Daytime Phone, in case we have a question about your order (   ) _____

Select one disk size: ___ 5.25-inch ___ 3.5-inch

Select your method of payment:

___ Check/Money Order enclosed (no cash please)

Figure your total cost:

Microsoft FORTRAN	$ _249.00_	___ Mastercard ___ Visa ___ American Express
Sales tax (see below for applicability)	$ _____	Card number _____
Freight charge	$ _7.50_	Expiration date _____
Total	$ _____	Cardholder's Signature _____

Allow 2-4 weeks for delivery upon receipt of this order coupon by Microsoft. Make checks payable to Microsoft. This offer is only valid in the 50 United States. Offer expires December 31, 1993. Your check will be deposited upon receipt. Credit card payments will be charged to your account upon shipment of your order. Add the applicable sales tax in the following states. AZ, CA, CO, CT, DC, FL, GA, HI, IA, ID, IL, IN, KS, KY, MA, MD, ME, MI, MN, MO, NC, NE, NJ, NM, NV, NY, OH, OK, PA, RI, SC, TN, TX, VA, WA, WI and WV. Microsoft reserves the right to correct sales tax rates and /or collect the sales tax assessed by additional states as required by law, without notice. No photocopies or facsimilies of this coupon will be accepted.

* Suggested retail price at the time of the printing of this coupon is $450.00. Microsoft reserves the right to change this price without notice.

Microsoft is a registered trademark of Microsoft Corporation.

FORTRAN Product Manager
Development Tools Division
Microsoft Corporation
One Microsoft Way
Redmond, WA 98052-9953